Not All Who Wander Are Over-thinking

Not All Who Wander Are Over-thinking

Candid Thoughts on Life, Beliefs, and Curiosity

SRIDHAR SACHIDANANDA

HAY HOUSE

HAY HOUSE INDIA
New Delhi • London • Sydney
Carlsbad, California • New York City

Hay House Publishers (India) Pvt Ltd
Muskaan Complex, Plot No. 3, B-2, Vasant Kunj, New Delhi – 110070, India

Hay House LLC, P.O. Box 5100, Carlsbad, CA 92018-5100, USA
Hay House UK Ltd, 1st Floor, Crawford Corner, 91-93 Baker Street, London W1U 6QQ, UK
Hay House Australia Publishing Pty Ltd, 18/36 Ralph St., Alexandria NSW 2015, Australia

Email: contact@hayhouse.co.in
Website: www.hayhouse.co.in

First published by Hay House India, 2025
10 9 8 7 6 5 4 3 2 1

ISBN 978-93-66115-75-7
ISBN 978-93-66116-68-6 (E-Book)

Printed at Replika Press Pvt Ltd

MIX
Paper | Supporting responsible forestry
FSC™ C016779

Hay House is committed to a sustainable future for our business, our readers and our planet. This book is made from Forest Stewardship Council® certified paper.

To my loving and forgiving family
that has tolerated me this long . . .

Contents

Section III: On Work

Section IV: On Lesson

Foreword

This is not a self-help book, though you might find it in a bookstore's self-help section. It is not an autobiography either. It is a book on life lessons I learnt and certain observations on life, work, and play that I deem worth sharing. I have lived a rather ordinary life—but I have had some thrilling and chilling experiences sporadically. My experiences range from inspirational to delusional.

I am not well-read or well-travelled, but even as a teenager, I was a seeker. When all my peers played cricket, I would climb rocks and trek evergreen forests for sport. I took a keen interest in yoga. I was a debating champion waxing eloquently on issues concerning grown-ups, not kids. But I never scored above 70 per cent marks in school. I have known since then that I march to the beat of a different drummer.

I have always felt like a misfit whatever the company I keep. It seems like other people want something very different from what I ask out of life. I am neither rich nor famous nor powerful. Nor do I not want any of these things. And if they are given to me, frankly, I don't know what I'd do with them.

I am still searching for the meaning of life. This is revealed to me in bits and pieces each time I do something new. I have always been a bit of a novelty-seeker who suffers from the 'next shiny thing' syndrome. I find it difficult to stick to an organisation, relationship, hobby, place, or even a daily routine. I am a wanderer. But not all who wander are lost.

This book, my debut, is all about the things I have learnt through self-inquiry. This journey began very early in life. All questions were asked by me to me, and the answers came as part of life experiences. I read Hugh Prather's Notes to Myself two decades ago and the inspiration for this book partly comes from it.

As I have tried to establish here, I am a tireless writer with some talent worth noticing. But the real intention of this book is to provoke thought, not convince the reader to do one thing or another. Our lives are the consequences of our choices. I will never do anything that takes away the right to choose from anyone. Certainly, not my readers.

There is nothing mystical in this book. The narrative is so simple that it will seem too 'simplistic' to be true. But if something in the book makes you say, 'Hey I know this, but I never thought of it this way!' then I have achieved my purpose in penning that essay. I have successfully provided a different perspective.

This book does not claim to provide a complete depth of understanding of anything. In fact, many of the essays end in a question. It merely seeks to spark wonder in the reader and inspire them to set off on their quest for self-knowledge, which I consider the basis for all life endeavours personal, worldly, and spiritual.

The choice of subjects is all common, everyday human experiences. The book seeks to delve a little deeper into such events that perplex us. It seeks not to 'enlighten' but to launch the reader on a lifelong journey of self-discovery. Safe journeys then . . . And thanks for choosing to read my book!

Section I

On Life

Grouping Instincts and First Impressions

When I want to join a group and participate in its activities, I wonder how to go about it. After years of experience in team building and working in groups, I am convinced the best approach is to look for similarities, not differences. When I focus on the similarities between 'them' and 'me', it becomes 'we'. It really is as simple as that.

When I look for similarities, the chasm between me and them closes, and the group becomes a set of homogenous, like-minded people. However, it is human nature to think of the differences first. The first thirty minutes spent in a new group are usually dedicated to identifying differences. It takes mindful effort to look for similarities.

Looking for differences is not a dreadful thing at all. In fact, it is an instinctive behaviour. It is my self-preservation instinct doing the math—fight, flight, or freeze. Seeking differences is a way of eliminating risks. Once that phase is over, commonalities come to the fore. Then one is ready to make the crucial decision: Stay or leave.

No two people are totally alike. There are bound to be differences within the same group and people have every right to hold on to their individual opinions. But it is the things that are common to all members of the group that keeps the group from falling apart. If the bond is strong, the group has resilience. If the bond is weak then disunity becomes a problem.

Personally, I am very picky about joining groups—online or offline. I first do some background research on what, why, and who of the group before approaching them for membership and participation. Then I request to be allowed to be part of the group for a few sittings. Unless I get such a firsthand experience, I don't normally decide whether to join or not.

If and when I join the group, I look for differences first and similarities later. It really depends on how much I like the people, not the individuals really, but the group as a whole. The opinions that I form concrete my decision to join or not.

However, during this process of evaluation, I must know whether the differences outnumber the similarities or vice versa. If the similarities are compelling, then I go right ahead and become a part of the group.

The process of rejecting the group is not so complicated at all. With just one sitting I get to know intuitively whether the group's membership is worth my time or not. If the group is not for me, I don't bother to go back seeking admission.

But similarities are what makes my time in the group worthwhile. Similarities make my participation meaningful. Similarities fetch me new friends and experiences. Being with similar people makes me happy. I have had many such experiences before becoming reclusive.

Summarily, one needs to make the effort to look for similarities and not just differences when wanting to join a group. Without looking for similarities, one may lose out on an opportunity to gain new friends and experiences.

The Truth about Lies

The truth about lying is that it is futile. The truth I write about here is not the biblical connotation of the word which is godly. The 'ultimate truth' that is extolled in so many ways in scriptures of all world religions—God is the only truth, etc. For the purpose of this article, I will restrict myself to the virtue of being true in word and deed, which is a moral that almost all loving parents inculcate in their children. Here, truthfulness means not uttering lies.

But why is lying futile? It is so because when I lie, it does not end there. Not only do I have to lie a second time to cover up for the first one and a third time to cover up for the first and second lies and then again and again till the truth is discovered. I reach a threshold beyond which lying fails to work. And I realise that no one will ever trust me like they did before the lying began. I become a serial liar.

And most often, the truth does come out eventually and the person who has been manufacturing lies to cover up the truth will be exposed. So now, do you really think that lying is worth all the trouble? Not only do you have to get more and more creative at lying but also remember every word of the lie that you uttered. Or you will get caught. And people mistrusting you is the least of your worries when certain lies land you in jail!

Let me give you a personal example. I was working for an IT company several years ago, and I lied to my boss about attending a training session. I had overslept that day and missed the session. When my boss called me and asked, I lied, telling him that I had attended the session. Little did I know that the facilitator of the session was my boss himself. He was the trainer for the session.

Can you imagine how embarrassed I was when I found this out from a colleague who attended the session? I immediately went up to my boss and confessed I had lied and told him the truth. That day, the respect and confidence that my boss had in me was flushed down the drain. This was a turning point for me.

However, this does not mean I have not uttered lies since then. I may have; I can't recall. But I have not locked myself into a situation where no amount of truthfulness can repair broken trust. I dare say that I have been largely truthful.

I read somewhere that there are two kinds of honesty—absolute and transactional. With my friends and family, I am absolutely honest. With the rest of the world, I am transactionally honest. This way I don't have to keep a log of all the lies I utter and invent new lies to cover previous ones. Perhaps the worst kind of lies we tell are the ones we tell ourselves.

Scepticism Meets Prayer

All my life, I have felt that the power of prayer is overrated. Millions across the world pray daily, but how many of those prayers are answered? Whenever family conventions force me to seek blessings from the Almighty, I confess I go through the motions—appeasing elders without the faintest hope in my heart that my prayer will be answered. Perhaps, I am yet to experience a miracle—an instance where I have prayed, and it is answered indeed.

Forgive my cynicism, but I have the detestable habit of speaking my mind.

Recently, however, my eighty-six-year-old father underwent dental surgery. He was in excruciating pain afterwards and had not slept for three days. I prayed for him. I did not go down on my knees or do something as filmy, but I prayed silently and sincerely in my mind, wishing for my father's pain to subside. And it happened almost instantly.

My father's pain became tolerable, and he slept like a baby for the rest of the day. Maybe it was the extra dose of painkiller that he was given. Either way, the desired outcome was achieved. My prayer for my father, which lasted no more than ten seconds, was fruitful. For the first time in my fifty-three years, a prayer of mine felt answered. I was overjoyed.

All this got me thinking. Why do countless prayers around the world go unanswered? Why does their suffering continue? Maybe it is because there is no sincerity in their prayers. And conversely, why do people have so much faith in prayer even when they do not get what they want?

Let me explain.

My prayer for my father worked. But if I had prayed for something for myself, would it have worked like a charm? Probably not. Does that mean the love I have for my father is the key? Do the prayers we say for the ones we love and those who care for us have a better capacity to manifest into miracles? I wonder. Does that mean the prayers I say for my well-being have lesser value? Is letting go of the self the key to successful praying? Praying for something bigger than myself?

Or is it all 'the power of positive thinking,' which is more dubious an aphorism than the 'power of prayer'? Simply thinking positively does not solve any problem. Following it up with affirmative action does. It is the right strategy that wins the game; not wishful daydreaming.

When does a prayer for me manifest into a solution to my predicament? I feel while a prayer does not come with any guarantee, it gives rise to hope for those in hopeless situations. It is like a drowning man clutching onto a straw and his faith forces him to think of alternatives and workarounds, like hanging on to a wooden log that is floating beside him.

One of those wildcard ideas clicks and voila! There is a way out. All kinds of prayer are founded on a belief system, and belief in agony can often resemble an overactive imagination. This is the key to the impenetrable door—imagination followed by visualisation of a solution.

Prayer, perhaps, is like a prompt on your computer screen. The ideas that follow shape your life story. So, pray as much as you want. It costs nothing, and if you are sincere, it may just open your mind to new possibilities.

After all, prayer calms the mind. And a calm mind can find solutions to almost anything.

Diet, Conscience, and the Question of Sin

Man is the only animal whose desire increases as he is fed. Lions, tigers, and all other predators hunt only for food. Humans are the only animal species that kills for sport. All these are outdated 'motherhood' statements as we call them in journalism, things that everyone knows (motherhood statements resemble statements like the Sun rising in the east). So, what's new?

Come to think of it, humans are the only animal species that exhibit this vice called greed. A lioness will peacefully drink from a watering hole with a gazelle a few feet away when she, and her cubs, are adequately fed. But man kills for entertainment. I am fortunate I live in a country like India where hunting wildlife is totally banned, whatever the motive—food or sport. It is punitive with severe punishment. And I am vegetarian.

Why do people get greedy even when all food is packed hygienically, delivered to the doorstep at a reasonable price, and even cooked freshly and served? Why the need to kill with their own hands? Is there some perverse, psychopathological motive? The need to shed blood? Or is it just good taste in food?

If you approach the subject of veganism from an evolutionary standpoint, you find that man always kills creatures that are far lower in the evolutionary timeline—Chicken, sheep, goats, fish, cattle, swine etc. Never a lion or a tiger or an elephant. These creatures attack people when threatened.

So, man goes for the low-hanging fruit and kills defenceless animals. I have seen people drag a herd of sheep to slaughter during festivals. They drag one sheep by the front leg, and the others follow without realising that their end is hopelessly near.

It is scientifically proven that man does not need to kill animals for food. I have been a vegetarian for fifty-three years, and I am not dead or underfed. I get all that I need from the protein, vitamins, fat, carbohydrates, minerals, and fibre in vegetables, cereals, pulses, and greens. I am as strong as a non-vegetarian and more resistant to disease and decay.

I am not trying to convert non-vegetarian people to vegetarianism here. This is not a crusade. I am only questioning the validity of being non-vegetarian when vegetarian food has all the required nourishment needed for the human body with almost no adverse side effects of consuming a given kind of diet.

Ultimately, non-veganism is a lifestyle choice. There is nothing 'sinful' about it and it is permitted by the law of the land. But if you have a conscience, then you might want to switch to vegetarianism. Because any way you look at it, killing is a sin.

Breaking Free from Self-Pity

I feel that the worst mental state to be in is to feel sorry for oneself. Self-pity is common among people who are disappointed for one reason or another. They curse their fates, complain that people have wronged them, and feel jealous of others who are happy with their lives. They waste time meant for living the life they have envisioned for themselves, wallowing in self-pity.

When that happens, life really gets worse. All that negativity in their minds sabotages what could normally be a happy life. It takes the joy of living and replaces it with depression. In psychology, depression is commonly defined as a feeling of hopelessness, worthlessness, and helplessness. I am pretty sure everyone who is reading this has felt so at some point in their life.

Life does deal a bad hand every now and again. Disappointments are common. But when a person is not resilient, it can be overwhelming. The feeling of not being in control and powerless can shatter even the most hopeful. Let me explain, as I always do, with a personal example.

When I catch myself feeling sorry for myself, I create a diversion—something positive to keep my mind occupied. Like watching a documentary on TV. The prospect of learning something new and unknown often lifts my spirits.

But mostly, I write. I give my mind something to think about—usually positive thoughts. I take a 5-km walk. I read. I call a friend who has not been in touch just for chitchat. I start living life and not just brooding.

This is similar to what a commando does when he encounters a hostage situation where there is only one entry or exit. He lobs a tear gas shell to create a diversion and breach the hostage environment. He shoots down the hostage takers before they can get him. Get the point?

The point is, when a diversion is created, the terrorist is instinctively trying to save his own life and forgets about the hostages for a few seconds. That is the window our hero needs to gun him down and free the hostages. Make disappointment and self-pity your terrorist enemy.

Do try it. It works for me. Every time you are self-pitying, stop and create a diversion. Anything at all. It could be your daily work or something not stressful or strenuous. Something light-hearted and enjoyable.

Like going outdoors and watching birds or strangers in the park. Writing a poem. Catching up on the news online. You will find that the negativity generated by self-pity will diminish with every passing minute and you will feel confident again to do the things you have to do that day.

This strategy works for varying expectations for all people and all negativity-generating situations. The key is to remember to use it when you are down for whatever reason. And once it works, it is yours forever.

Creating diversions is not a great art or science. It is how the human mind works. When you lose someone to bereavement, the average time you spend in mourning is thirteen days in

India. Then you get back to your work, life, and play. Because you crave change. You want your life back.

Similarly, you can rid yourself of self-pity and depressive feelings anytime you want because the very same craving for change propels you find alternatives to lighten your mood, fill you with positivity, and help you recover. If you are depressed, find your diversionary tactic now!

Overcoming Paranoia

I have experienced paranoia in many forms. It is simply devastating and traumatic to go through and survive a paranoid episode. But for most people, it passes, and almost all paranoid personalities experience extended non-episodic periods.

Paranoia results in social withdrawal. The person is likely to avoid interpersonal interaction because of fear that they might be ridiculed, attacked, maimed, and a host of other non-existent threats that normal people laugh at.

For the paranoid person, the threat perception seems, or rather is, very real and stymieing. Sometimes, the perceived threat feels so unbearable that the patient is driven to suicide to escape the pain.

My paranoid episodes lasted close to twenty-five years of my life. I am overjoyed to state the fact that I have not experienced a single episode in the last five years. This episode-free part of my life has been the most fulfilling time of all. I am just as normal as other people. I have created so much content in these five years and led an inspired, productive, and happy life.

Therapy and medication certainly helped. But what brought about this amazing transformation was actually self-awareness. After many years of paranoia and trying to identify triggers—life situations that cause it—I am finally free of this excruciatingly painful affliction.

Knowing how to react to a given situation and acquiring the skills to avoid or survive such situations that have historically precipitated an episode, is critical for a paranoid personality.

When I encounter people or situations that are unavoidable, it is necessary for me to question my delusive beliefs. I remember one of my favourite therapists who helped me for over two decades commending me for being the 'most insightful patient I have seen in his thirty-one years of practice'.

Questions like: 'Is this person really dangerous?' 'What is the worst that can happen to me?' 'Am I really in danger or is it just in my head?' 'How would a normal person react to this kind of a situation?' 'What happened to me when I felt the same kind of fear before?' 'Did I get admitted or hang in there till it passed?' 'How would I rate the intensity of this fearful experience on a scale of 1–5?' (one being bearable and five being intense). 'Am I really so important that people should want to harm me?'

In other words, I try to stay in touch with reality using logic rather than emotion. And usually, when the symptoms subside, I feel like a winner and mighty relieved. But all this is easier said than done.

I know how a paranoid person's brain works. Logic alone is insufficient. Winning strategies like cognitive behavioural therapy (CBT), medication, admissions to mental institutions, observation and treatment for at least fifteen days is not just recommended, but ideal. If one utterly understands paranoia and the accompanying anguish, they will be open to seeking help.

Paranoid episodes can really leave a person mentally drained and dysfunctional. Additionally, residual symptoms can last for months. However, people like me who are self-aware take mental notes each time we experience an episode. And we use our intelligence to analyse and understand what occurs during the episode.

We make a list of triggers and stay clear of them. And above all, I don't despair. I remain hopeful that all the pain is transient. I am not the powerless person that my mind is making me feel. I am stronger than that. And this, too, shall pass.

Breaking the Chains of Self-Doubt

It is common for everyone to suffer from self-doubt from time to time. The thing about self-doubt is that the outcome of my actions is uncertain till the very end of the episode. Only time will tell.

Whether I win or quit midway or even before I begin, depends on how much I believe in myself and how much energy I bring to my work. I wish there were an easier, softer way to know the fallout—success or failure—but there is no other way to begin, stick, and make it work.

I could statistically calculate the risk and predict possible outcomes. But as the statisticians themselves say, there are three kinds of lies—statistics, statistics, statistics. They are somewhat true when the survey sample size is huge, but on a personal level, they tend to be misleading.

Self-doubt is like a dormant parasite that dwells in my mind and is activated when I am doing something vital, challenging, or new. The greater the expectations of me, the more that self-doubt.

I fear that people will judge me based on my past actions and remember the negative vibes I attracted from them. Or that I am constitutionally incapable of the task at hand, or the circumstances are against, not in favour.

I believe I don't have the grit and mettle to achieve it. I fear I will be mocked and castigated if I try and fail. You even feel that all that is not worth even a feeble attempt. I fear risk.

The more you analyse self-doubt, it grows with the feeling of 'no can do'. Thinking positively in such a scenario, as many self-help books advise, seems like a highly naïve solution to a very complex human dilemma. The diffidence grows to a point where it envelops your mind with negativity that is highly crippling.

Is there a way out of this? There are simple things one can do. Aim small, miss small. This is the one time-tested strategy snipers are trained in. Thinking big sounds romantic. But all great human endeavours begin small and grow. Most success stories are preceded by repetitive trials and errors that were carried out in people's garages. Like the prolific inventor Thomas Alva Edison said, 'I have not failed. I have discovered 10,000 ways it won't work.'

Or you can ask for help. Finding and getting like-minded people excited enough about your ideas and asking them to join you in the journey. Be careful to pick the ones that have the capabilities you lack. Give them freedom, share your resources, and reward them for their effort when you win. If you lose, ensure that there is no bad blood between you and them. Keep the faith.

Finally, dare! This is what entrepreneurs do. Your level of commitment is directly proportional to your chances of success. If you do not have the conviction required to get the job done, do not commit. This does not sound like a winning strategy but only you know best.

You could, however, not abandon the idea forever. You could try when the entry-level odds are low, and you get time to build from ground up with renewed confidence and vigour.

As long as I am clear of the what, why, when, and where, the who and how will fall into place when the time is right. I just need to sit tight and not let go of my grand dreams.

Stop Managing Expectations, Live the Life You Want

If you think about it particularly, you will discover that you have been trying hard to manage people's expectations of you for most of your life. In childhood, you have to live up to the expectations of your parents, siblings, and other elders in the family. As a teenager, you were compelled to live up to the expectations of your teachers and peers. As an adult, you struggle to manage the expectations of your customers, bosses, co-workers, spouse, and children. In a nutshell, life becomes a fight to maintain people's expectations of you.

In the melee, when do you have time to live your life and meet your expectations of yourself? Each of us has 'some' idea of what to become and how to lead our lives—aspirations, plans, action items. In truth, people are not working, loving, achieving, or playing, they are forever meeting the expectations of other people.

Stop reading this for a moment and give it serious thought and you will certainly agree. This tendency to seek the approval of others and please them begins in early childhood and can last a lifetime for most of us. When do we really take time off to please ourselves? Late in life, when death is knocking on our door?

I say that if you are reading this, then you are ready to pay some attention to yourself. Make a list of the achievements in life so far in one column. In the second column make notes about why you achieved these things—more importantly to please whom—yourself or other people. If you have done it for others, then it is most likely that the achievement has brought you little happiness. Now decide whether you would do it all over again for yourself . . . and how different.

Also, make a list of achievements that you have not been able to accomplish so far. And go after them . . . for your own sake. Would that fetch you joy? A sense of accomplishment? Happiness? Can you dream of a life where you are not accountable to anybody for your actions (as long as you are not breaking the law)?

Let me cite an example. I know someone who slogged in various tech companies till the age of forty-five years. He is now semi-retired and does things voluntarily, without any charge. It gives him satisfaction to know that he is making a difference in people's lives. This is his reward, and he does not ask for more. He is setting a fine example. He is content knowing that come what may, his actions are unquestionable and that widens and deepens his life experiences and benefits others as well.

There is not much you can do about what other people think of you and your actions. It is not in your control. So, why bother anyway? If you have lived a fulfilling life according to your expectations, then keep at it. In today's world, no one really cares for others. Sometimes even family can become distant. All that matters is whether you have lived life the way you envisioned it, or not.

Living Simply and Simply Living

What is the difference between living simply and simply living? First, a working definition of both—living simply is to reduce to bare bones, discretionary spending, and moderation. Living simply helps you focus on important things that fetch joy, comfort, satisfaction, and a sense of belonging. The key is to decide what these things are. Living simply does not mean you have to settle for second best. You just need to have time and money for the best when you really need them.

It involves sacrifices, at least in the beginning, and then it becomes a habit and embeds itself into your very DNA. It streamlines existence in a way that saves time and money and optimises consumption. Living simply is not frugal. Life need not become boring or spartan. You need to allot time and resources to things that really matter. The need-want dichotomy is in play here.

In a word, simply living is vegetating—leading a purposeless life. It means thoughtlessly going through the motions without ambition, goals, inspiration, or direction. Simply living is eating, watching TV, sleeping, and repeating. I tried this for some time and detested it.

Here, the day ends when banal needs are gratified and there is nothing more to look forward to. Even pets have a rigid routine. They crave food and exercise at the same time each day. But a simply living human doesn't need even that. This is a tragedy. This person lives to die . . . such as waste.

Playing the devil's advocate here: I would rather die risking my health and finances as opposed to simply living. Life zips past me. Why waste it? Happiness always follows achievement—unless it's a victory in a bloody war. A purposefully led life is something to be proud of when I am old and grey. It fetches fulfilment. I must work, play, and be among people rather than die bored and lonely.

There is so much life has to offer—love, affluence, influence, learning, divine inspiration, friendship—the list is limited only by one's desires. Ask and thou shalt receive. The universe will make me worthy of the gift and then voila!

Living simply is aspiring to ideal situations, enjoying them by merit. Simply living is a pathological affliction among people who want to survive rather than live.

The Beauty in the Ordinary

At times I feel sorry for myself for having led an ordinary life. What I miss the most is the kind of travel experiences that I desire. I never had the means for it anyway. But having led an ordinary life is nothing to be ashamed of. At my current age, I have a sense of fulfilment and contentment. I envy well-travelled people. They have a lot more life experience than I have.

For me, living an ordinary life is okay if I am at peace with myself, enjoy good health, and have some savings for retirement. An ordinary life is okay if I have extraordinarily strong bonds with friends and family.

An ordinary life is okay if I have helped some people in distress and come up with solutions that make their lives bearable. For me, living a purposeful life filled with meaning is more important than touring all the hotspots in the world. This may sound like the fox and sour grapes fable, but it is true that I really am content with my lot.

Living an ordinary life is okay when I achieve feats such as this book. I finished writing it on time and honoured my commitment to the publisher. For me, it is something to be proud of. Something that deserves praise.

There are many people who travel widely and wish to write about their travels. But they cannot actually do so or never get down to doing it. I ghost-wrote a book such as this for a person who has served in Europe and Africa. I recounted his experiences in the book for remuneration. It was then I realised how lucky I was though the experiences were not mine.

Living an ordinary life is okay if you can make other people's lives feel special to them. If you can assist in making life more meaningful for them. I have done that as a teacher. I have helped many young people get internships and coached them in building successful careers in mass communication and journalism. For me, this is an achievement that deserves to be acknowledged worthy.

Living an ordinary life is okay if I have faced and emerged victorious in extraordinary circumstances, crossed paths with extraordinary people, learnt extraordinary life lessons, and developed at least one extraordinary skill. Living an ordinary life is okay if I have known love and I am loved.

Not everyone leads an extraordinary life. What makes life extraordinary is their attitude. I can complain and be miserable or enjoy the gifts I have and be happy. If everyone is extraordinary, then who is ordinary? As I have mentioned somewhere in this book, it is the ordinary people who validate and acclaim the greatness of extraordinary people with their awe.

This is a book about a person who has led an ordinary life—me. By my own measure, the life I have lived is quite ordinary. What makes this book special—not extraordinary, mind you—is that I wrote it and you are reading it.

The Childlike Joy in Growing Older

I wonder why people colour their hair and opt for anti-ageing therapies. Ageing is universal and irreversible. It is not such a bad thing after all. I want to age gracefully. I don't colour my grey hair and beard. When I lose all my hair, I will not get a hair transplant, and I certainly will not want to undergo any anti-ageing therapy.

I am fifty plus, and I let it show—proudly. As I age, I feel more at peace with myself. The best thing about ageing is that you get more time for yourself. You reconcile and accept your limitations. You don't go chasing mirages. People lower their expectations of you. This gives you time to do the things that you really want.

With age comes wisdom and self-awareness. I am clearer about what I want or don't want. Age has mellowed me. I was very ambitious and aggressive as a young man. Now, I am patient and tolerant because I have no need for aggression. I am not fighting anybody or anything. I choose my battles with people.

Age brings with it many gifts. The most valuable one for me is the ability to let go—letting go of resentments, regrets, depressing thoughts, harmful obsessions, and toxic people. It also diminishes unhealthy habits and replaces them with healthy, empowering ones.

Life has started to slow down, allowing me proper rest and time for reflection. It is very much like the clear skies after a storm. I find peace, fulfilment, and companionship. I can now afford to indulge in the simple pleasures of life like pursuing a hobby or travelling.

Age also brings with it fond memories and the recognition or reputation that you have earned in society. And if you are physically, mentally, and financially independent, then ageing is the best thing that has ever happened to you.

In response to people who believe that age is just a number, and does not stop them from doing anything, I say that I totally agree. If you are active and useful, that is a bonus for you.

Younger cohorts come to me for help and advice. Having gained much work and life experience, I am in a better position to help them now more than ever. This, in turn, inspires better output from them. They trust me to guide them, and I must. Ageing is not something that scares me. It is becoming useless that does.

When you actually come to think of it, age makes people childlike. They are set in their ways but for the ones who have the means and the inclination, it can be a lot of fun like childhood. With fewer responsibilities, you can enjoy life with renewed curiosity and energy just like children do.

You can do things that you never knew you were capable of albeit moderately and maturely; not recklessly. You can make new friends, join a yoga group or a gym, explore spirituality, read, write, and immerse yourself in social service—the list is endless. All because you have the time and the means as you age. The only condition to be met is that you stay healthy, sane, and independent.

Freedom Fuels Happiness

Happiness means different things to different people. For me, true happiness is freedom—to live my life the way I choose. I want good health and freedom from disease. I want financial freedom and independence.

I want freedom from a taxing schedule and time to entertain myself with those things that make me happy. I want the freedom to choose the people I spend time with. I want absolute freedom to script my life the way I want.

Gurus and life coaches complicate things and describe happiness in convoluted ways. According to me, all this is quite unnecessary. Happiness is simply the freedom to exercise free will the way you want. If I make a list of the instances when I have been unhappy, I find that, in such times, my freedom was curtailed either by circumstances or people.

When I began my career in journalism, the only job offer I received was for a part-time correspondent position in a distant, small, and unimportant town. It was a very low-paying job, and I had to struggle to make ends meet.

I could have chosen to refuse the job and wait for a while until a better opportunity came along. But those were times when my family was going through a tough phase financially. Every rupee mattered. So, I was forced to take up the job and make a beginning.

It is true that I got better opportunities later in my career, but the humble beginning did not give me the right leverage to bargain for better pay and emoluments. Career-wise, I have never had such leverage. It has been desperate job-hopping all the way. I have always taken what came my way with limited freedom to shape my career the way I imagined.

In contrast, if I had got the right launch pad, I would have been in a better position to clinch better jobs. I would have made the kind of friends who matter in sculpting a better career. I would have been happy.

I am not cursing my lot here or whining that I have been victimised. I have been super lucky in my personal life and relationships. I have no complaints in that department. I am grateful and happy for all the luxuries of life that I enjoy today. I just used my first job as an example to explain how important freedom is to being happy.

Being happy is being truly free. Free in every sense. Being fit, contented, grateful, inspired to create, having true friends, finding love, leading a purposeful life, and I realise nothing in this list is beyond my control. This means that being happy is actually in my own hands.

The moment I give up my freedom and let someone else or a circumstance control me, I become unhappy. Happiness is doing what I want and being who I want to be. But when I am overwhelmed by people and situations controlling my life, I fight. I fight for liberty to live free. Such a battle is lofty.

Loving Oneself

I was a regular at a gym many years ago. There was a poster in the changing room that read: 'Falling in love with yourself allowed here!' That provoked some thoughts that I present here.

If you don't love yourself then you are approval-seeking. This is worse than narcissism. If you are dependent on others for strokes, you have chosen to relinquish your autonomy to them. You are but a puppet on strings.

Approval-seeking behaviour is shackling. It limits the possibility of achievement. It ties you down to the whims of others who then play havoc with your life and derive sadistic pleasure out of causing you pain. I have been there and, trust me, it is a demeaning and crushing experience.

This is not a discussion that supports megalomania, but natural kindness and patience with myself do wonders for my sanity, building self-confidence. The ask is to objectively look at my actions and question if all that I can possibly do has been done to get things right in any situation.

If yes, then I am a winner, and no awards are needed from others. I can sleep better at night knowing that certain circumstances are not in my grasp and let events take their natural course.

The first step is acceptance—accepting things about yourself that cannot be changed. Then demonstrating the courage to change the things you can. Lastly, the wisdom to know the difference between the two (Serenity Prayer).

Approval-seeking behaviour begins in early childhood where a strict upbringing coupled with stress on humility and self-deprecation as virtues exist. Later it's because of rejection by teachers, peers, and the opposite gender. Then bosses and co-workers. Finally, one's own flesh and blood—if you are heavily dependent on them for approval.

Only a firm and unwavering faith in myself and my abilities can cure me of this malady. When I perceive each little victory or savour success as a product of my personality, I develop healthy self-respect.

When that happens, I don't need others to tell me I am good. A little compassion with myself when I fail and affectionate appreciation when I succeed is in order. That is the prescription for freedom from want of attention from others.

I can be whole without appreciation from others. I will survive even if I am marooned on the island called loneliness if I draw deep from the well of inexhaustible life-giving water called self-respect. Being mediocre and self-sufficient is not a sin. I am what I am.

Love, Marriage . . . Or Staying Single

'Insanity is doing the same things over and over again, expecting different results.' I believe this quote is attributed to Albert Einstein and later mystery writer Rita Mae Brown. Be that as it may, I find this definition of insanity the most accurate, articulate, and revealing. Certain things that I have done in my life prove the veracity of this statement.

First, some FAQ of my life. I am fifty-three years old and have never been married. It was not that I did not want to get married or did not try to get married. Each intimate relationship with a girl that I got into, sooner than later, became chaotic and unbearable for both of us. I finally realised that enough was enough. In hindsight, this is probably the best decision I have ever made.

I am not a jilted lover. I have no regrets whatsoever about being unwedded. Leading a peaceful life today, I feel that I did the right thing by staying single. If I had married, these marriages would have come with an extremely short expiry date. I really feel that I have done myself and women, in general, a big favour by staying single.

But why the reference to insanity? Because I was insanely trying to find the ideal woman and wife. I was smitten by the idealism and wanted the relationship to be perfect in every way. When it came to disagreements, I was angry and confused. I lacked maturity and insight into what makes marriages successful. Maybe I should have asked around and emulated other people who are happy in their marriages. But no. I had to figure it all by myself through painful trial and error.

Romantic relationships confuse me even now. Though I know that I have the capacity to infinitely love my family I was born into and live with now. In order to find peace, I had to completely let go of the romantic ideal of love and marriage. I had to stay single. And staying single is not so bad after all.

Many of my married friends envy the freedom that I enjoy. I react sharply when people treat me like someone who is miserable. On the contrary, I now lead a peaceful, comfortable, and inspired life. Thanks to the one decision to be single, the madness ended a long time ago.

I sympathise with my married friends who are struggling to make ends meet in a world which has become overly complicated and competitive. They are always discussing how to pay their kids' school and private tuition fees.

You probably think that I am the most self-centred man on earth. No, I do care for friends and family. I am not the devil's advocate preaching the merits of remaining single. I am thankful that I have fewer needs than married people do.

My life is definitely not as complicated as theirs. I respect, even admire, couples who try hard to make their marriages work. Being single does not mean that I am cynical about love and marriage. I simply and very decisively know that that they won't work for me.

Goodwill vs Gain

Given the choice, would you choose goodwill or gain? To gain the goodwill of others, one must help them in their time of need or simply be a friend to them when they are forsaken by everyone else. Goodwill often leads to gain. However, a business transaction not based on goodwill leads to only monetary gain and nothing beyond that. Goodwill is lasting. Money comes and goes.

Goodwill is often a happenstance. It is earned when people support each other. The dynamics of demand and supply govern business. However, a business connection that lasts long enough can often make way for goodwill between the parties involved.

Goodwill creates mutual dependence. Business for gain creates material wealth based on the value of goods and services. Goodwill is based on the unwritten covenant that 'I will be there for those who depend on me' and vice versa. Business is based on a contract.

To get business I need to pitch and showcase my capabilities. To earn goodwill, I must help people facing difficulties.

Goodwill can often cause gain. But a transaction motivated by pure gain rarely causes goodwill.

So, what would you choose? Goodwill or gain? I desire both. After all, I have established that the duo is not mutually exclusive. I win a bonus when what is meant to be a pure business transaction makes way for a lasting relationship. I cannot measure goodwill in terms of money.

Goodwill often generates repeat business. When a customer trusts me to deliver the goods on time, as per specifications, he gives me more business. In such a case making money should be on the backburner.

Preserving goodwill is key; even if it means that you suffer a loss from that transaction. It is okay to break even in a transaction based on goodwill and not make any profit. It is the relationship that matters not the money. Since this is simply good karma, I am certain to make my money elsewhere. No need to fret.

Business ensures daily sustenance. Goodwill is the safety net that catches when I fall. Business drives me. Goodwill saves me. There are several variables to factor in business. With goodwill, there is only one consideration—mutual trust and respect. I can shut down an unprofitable venture and launch another one. But goodwill is fragile, the relationship can end forever if the trust is broken.

Being Grateful for What I Have

People often complain more than they should. Their grumbling is a result of a feeling that they have been wronged in some way or given a raw deal. They whine that providence or other people have unfairly treated them. They claim that they deserve more . . . that life gave them a lemon when they asked for a diamond. They should, perhaps, learn how to make lemonade and sell it.

The point is, every soul on earth is given not just anxiety and deprivation, but countless things that empower them to make their lives happier however poor and under-privileged they may be. Consider these gross estimates:

- According to World Population Review, 1,66,859 people will die each day worldwide in 2024, which is roughly two people every second. If you are reading this, then you are lucky to be alive.
- According to a report published by the International Labor Organization (ILO), during the pandemic, 235.21 million people lost their jobs worldwide. If you still have one, be grateful.

- According to World Population Review (2024), Pakistan has approximately eight million homeless people. If you have a roof over your head and a family that loves you, consider yourself blessed.
- Approximately, one in nine men and one in twelve women succumb to cancer according to the International Agency for Research on Cancer (IARC). If you are healthy, active, and independent, be satisfied.
- As of 2020, globally, approximately forty-three million people were either born blind or lost sight according to the International Agency for Prevention of Blindness (IPAB). Well, you are reading this book, aren't you?

What makes life more enjoyable are the fundamental necessities—good health, home, job, family, and even free will. Everybody deserves all this because being born comes with an inalienable human right to be able to enjoy these privileges. And gratitude is what makes the enjoyment of these rights meaningful by adding dignity to life.

When I count my blessings and not my troubles, I am contented. Most of my worries stem from my feeling of over-entitlement. The feeling that I deserve more than I receive. From my perspective, this is correct. But the universe has the ominous responsibility of maintaining balance. The universe's decision is unquestionable, and there isn't a damn thing I can do to change that.

Sometimes, I believe that I deserve more. Such a feeling is not criminal. If it makes me work harder towards my goals, then 'want' is better than 'need'. If that feeling inspires me towards extraordinary achievement, then nothing could be better. I am blessed. I am not common, I am special.

However, if it makes me compare my lot to that of successful people and feel inferior, unlucky, and cheated, then this negative emotion can stymie me. I will spend a lifetime playing the victim, whining and complaining instead of aspiring and achieving success. Life is too short to be wasted on such a useless, pointless, wasteful pursuit.

In conclusion, whatever my lot, I am grateful for the blessings I have received. I work hard towards acquiring those attributes that I lack so that I may enjoy the fruits of my labour. That is the entire lesson in *karma* in a nutshell for me. My calling is that of a writer and a storyteller. If I have convinced you with this piece, then I certainly deserve more.

Riding the Highs and Lows

If you are bipolar like me, you will understand this essay better. Being manic has its drawbacks. You tend to lose all inhibitions, abuse substances, and go overboard with what you say and do. If it is not alcohol or narcotics, it is binge-shopping or binge-eating.

But the kind of momentum you get with your pet projects when you are manic is unmatched. Ideas flow unabated. Racy thoughts, as they are called in psychiatry, result in amazing insights that can be converted into convincing arguments for a chapter of my book.

I skip between racing thoughts that could be recorded by writing them down to be analysed when I am normal. They provide insight, unbridled by inhibition, self-criticism, or criticism from others. They are pure thoughts, untainted by opinion.

A lot of people with very little understanding confuse bipolar and bisexual. That is a joke by the way. But they are not my concern in penning this article. I want to demonstrate that being bipolar means being above-average in creativity and how using momentum during a manic stage can convert ideas that occur in the mind into something of value. Vincent van Gogh was diagnosed as bipolar. His still-life painting of the flower vase sold for USD 22 million at an auction.

Being manic can be a curse when you are with people, especially too many strangers. Your behaviour can become unpredictable, offending, and unsavoury. This is why you must avoid all human contact when you are manic.

When you are depressed, the same rule applies. Isolate yourself because you are prone to delusional thinking, and paranoia, and are less authentic in interpersonal interactions. Suffice it to say that both extreme states of a bipolar person are better experienced in isolation, devoid of human contact. Without losing heart, know that for most people, these states are temporary—they pass with time, and you will return to your usual cheerful self again, eager for company.

But how do I use this time in isolation? Do I sleep it off? Or do I spend it brooding and feeling miserable? Feeling sorry for myself? If I am hypomanic, then it is an opportunity for me to create.

Content, painting, poem, blog, or whatever I like. I am naturally more articulate when I am manic. More creative is a better way of describing it. I think of ideas less thought of before. I become seminal in my thinking.

When I am depressed, it is extremely challenging to focus. The lows are infinitely worse than the highs. They come with delusions that affect rational thinking. I experience much pain and a sense of abandonment. A sense of hopelessness, worthlessness, and helplessness can be overwhelming.

When that happens, like a drowning man grasping for a straw. I fight to stay sane. Creating may not be possible in such a state of mind. I let go of everything until I am better.

But the work I do when I am manic is my beacon. The creations that emerge from mania and the compulsiveness to write give me a reason to be happy. They are the antithesis of what I feel when I am down under. They show me the way to live life—exuberantly.

The Luck Conundrum

What exactly is luck? It is just another word for timing. If you are in the right place, at the right time, with the right people, you are lucky. If the place, timing, or people are wrong, then you are unlucky. This definition of luck makes it circumstantial and less deterministic. It also means that being lucky is a waiting game. You must wait for the right conditions to make your move.

This characterisation makes luck less a providential whim and puts the onus on the individual to be alert and constantly on the lookout for opportune occurrences. It also presupposes that lucky circumstances present themselves several times in one's lifetime. It is clearly up to the individual to realise when the time, place, and people are right for affirmative action.

But how does one know that the time, place, and people are right? This is where intuition comes into play. It is not something you 'figure out'. You just know it in your bones. Intuition is described as the ability to understand something instinctively, without the need for conscious reasoning.

Listening to that little voice in your head with all your heart will let you know when the harvest is ripe for the picking.

Providence gives everyone a second, even many, chance. Do not blame providence for your miseries if you have not utilised opportunities prudently.

I can think of at least half a dozen opportunities that I was given to improve my lot. If I have squandered and ended up a loser, I don't blame bad luck at birth. This is simply rationalising my stupidity.

The very same favourable circumstances—in varying forms—were presented to you again and again. But money, influence, and the good life these wonderful opportunities provide must make you grateful and industrious. Instead, if you become a slacker, grandiose, and derelict, it is you who wasted away the blessings. It is not bad luck at all. And it is also true that your loss was someone else's gain. Someone more deserving perhaps?

When a stroke of good luck or a windfall makes me grateful, I must consolidate my gains and build on them. There is nothing sinful in being a little indulgent with money when I can easily afford it. But when I take good luck for granted, I am doomed. That is when misfortune befalls me.

Nothing to Lose, Everything to Gain

I am fifty-three. I find myself at a crossroads. I survived my midlife crisis pretty well, and now I feel empty inside. The emptiness is partly being filled by authoring this book and taking up freelance assignments to keep myself occupied. But my daily dilemma is, what next?

If I were a spiritually oriented person, I could have explored organised religion more deeply. People tend to lean towards organised religion as they age. Right now, I am barely scratching the surface of my faith.

I could have got involved with non-profits and helped people in distress. But somehow such pursuits fail to keep me interested and committed in the long term. Though empty, I still find respite in—and am attracted to—reclusiveness.

But the one thing that I notice about my life today is that I have nothing to lose. Nothing that really matters . . . nothing so valuable that I cannot live without it. I will not go into the things that I have or lack. I have done that elsewhere in the book many times.

When I examine my daily life today closely, I am not doing things that other people do. Which means, by their understanding, I am nothing. But my argument is that I have nothing to lose.

I consider being in a nothing-to-lose situation highly empowering. This is a time to begin being afresh and do the things I have always dreamed of. It gives you an unassailable power to innovate. You can experiment with new things without worrying about losing a job, a partner, money, or a reputation. I have none of these now, and hence I can become whatever I choose to be.

I never really envisioned writing a book when I was in my thirties. I had no time even to toy with the idea. If I am able to do it in my fifties, when my brain is still sharp, then I must consider myself lucky.

Being in a nothing-to-lose position is actually a blessing. I can clean my slate and start scripting new chapters of my life. The journey is far more exciting when you have nothing to lose, as you can stray from the path and create your own.

When you have nothing to lose, you are the opposite of what people assume—powerless. I am more powerful than most people who fear failure and the loss of money, are beleaguered by divorces, and worry about losing their popularity in a scandal. By this kind of power, I mean personal power, not the kind that comes from wealth or fame.

This is a period of reconstruction for me—from the ground up. It is a phase of my life filled with introspection and re-engineering. I can now afford to tinker with the non-functioning aspects of my life and align my actions and lifestyle with my true desires. For the record, this book-writing endeavour has been one of the most fulfilling times of my entire life.

What's funny is that once I made up my mind to draft the first chapter, all the banal requirements of my life simply fell into place. Though I have nothing to lose, I now have everything

I could ordinarily want. Perhaps there is a lesson in that. As quoted in ancient Hindu scriptures, by renouncing everything—simply letting go—man attains everything he desires and what is lasting (and non-ephemeral).

Bargaining with the Divine

Should one bargain with God? For good fortune, or lesser life troubles? Bargaining for things we get is as old as humanit itself. It is the mother of all arts; the ancient foundation of commerce. Assume for a moment that you can bargain with God, your maker.

The disclaimer here is that I am not a believer. Faith is a gift I am yet to receive.

Since He created you and you do not exist till the moment He does, you cannot bargain with Him about things with which you are born. These things are 'non-negotiable,' and acceptance is key. All haggling must happen during your lifetime.

If God were to parley with me about the things that I desire or reject in life, what would be the topics of our negotiation? I would make two lists—things I want and those I detest.

Let us do the elimination process first—undesirable life events. Ill-health would be the first on my list. Then comes financial difficulty, strained relationships, and my worrying about things that may or may not happen.

However, am I not missing the point? If God does agree to totally remove sickness, poverty, family strife, and anxiety from my life, then I am free! Free to achieve, prosper, and fulfil all my earthly desires. But no! I say I want more.

I want 'divine grace' to be happy, too. I want God to provide me with good health, which is completely in my hands, and riches, a human construct, not godly because man invented wealth. Finally, lasting relationships, which is all about love—a human emotion that makes us give, not take.

Another angle is that life's trials are life lessons. What does not kill me, makes me stronger. Why should I shy away from life's many tribulations? If I look at trouble as a learning opportunity, I can enhance my self-awareness and function better in life, work, and play.

This is a compelling case against bargaining with God. Why bother Him when I do not need Him? If I no longer have troubles in life, and the life I live is picture-perfect, why must I work? Think of a scenario where all good fortune and life troubles are equally balanced—50–50. Would that be ideal in terms of comfort and life lessons? Maybe, I wonder . . .

The Illusion of Rehabilitation

I have seen the cheapest of rehabs, where homeless people (who become homeless because all their family and friends abandon them) are kept for rehabilitation and a few of the others that treat inmates respectfully and medically—viewing addiction as an illness.

I have seen addicts and alcoholics being thrashed to pulp and bleeding till they can no longer resist the 'treatment' given in 'down-market' rehabs. I have seen patients from affluent families being made to clean a toilet used by seventy-five people to make them understand what 'ego-subjugation' is.

I have known addicts being sodomised. I have seen people with grave mental issues being treated like animals because the people who run the rehab believe in a no-pain-no-gain philosophy. These people beat the addiction out of you.

All the resentment that comes with ill-treatment builds up into rage against the people who put you in rehab in the first place. The moment you are out, you are thirsting for revenge against your loved ones.

In the 'up-market' rehabs, the doctors and counsellors are kind, giving, empathetic, suave, and helpful. They serve decent food in these places and give you private rooms. They create conditions that convince the people who put you there (usually family and friends) that you are being treated well. There is no cause for worry.

You get all that you ordinarily want in such rehabs, from dark chocolate to cigarettes. And if you are rich enough to bribe your counsellor, two pegs of whiskey every now and then. But all this comes at a price. A hefty one—Rs 2,00,000 per month.

The thing about substance abuse rehabilitation is that it is pointless. If you are substance dependent, then it is for life. This is the ugly truth. I have known alcoholics who have been abstinent for 18–25 years and then relapse with the vengeance and drink to death to make up for all those years of abstinence. Yet, when they are in an AA meeting, former alkies introduce themselves as: 'I am so-and-so. I am an "alcoholic".' The reason is addiction is an illness, like hypertension and diabetes. Do you stop taking your medication if your heart rate or blood sugar is normal all of a sudden? No, you take them anyway.

I have known at least one alcoholic who relapsed after eighteen years of abstinence. He was in his sixties then. I figure he is dead by now, with all that 'making up' for lost drinking years.

The WHO has categorised alcoholism and addiction as the third-largest killer after heart ailments and diabetes. It is not a question of morality. It is pathological. An addiction that destroys families and careers is truly an affliction, not a 'character flaw'. Any good psychiatrist will tell you that.

There is no justification for drinking and using, no matter how convincing it sounds. Self-help groups, therapy, and medication can only do so much. But any way you look at it, rehabilitation as it is today, is a roaring business gambit. It is the only business where people spend large amounts of money knowing fully well that it is a scam and there are no guaranteed deliverables.

The funny thing is, some of the rehabs I have been to are owned and managed by former alcoholics and addicts. The others are by psychiatrists. This is a money-minting opportunity for a former alky or druggie to make enough money to compensate for all those years of their career spent drinking and using. And you fall for that?

I particularly remember meeting a very young boy in rehab a long time ago. He was a tenth-grade student who had been admitted to the facility for 'Facebook addiction'. Can you believe that?

Anyway, this kid, after spending a few months in a rehab overflowing with alcoholics and addicts, learnt so much, including drinking, shooting, snorting, smoking, vaping, sourcing the drug, lies to tell, places to hide the stuff, cheating people into give him cash, and many other ways substances are consumed. By the time his parents got him out, he had a master's degree in being an alcohol and narcotics addict.

Elders in India warn their children to be aware of 'jail friends' and 'rail friends'. They are never any good for anyone. And a rehab is the perfect place to make such 'great' friends.

The Two Pillars of Wellness

There are tons of reading materials on the Internet and in books on healthy habits to adopt. But I consider two of them the most important—staying hydrated and getting enough sleep.

These two habits have kept me active and free of sickness. I am not a doctor or a nutritionist. However, from personal experience, I have figured out that these two habits have made me almost immune to diseases. I rarely fall sick.

I drink water every waking hour, which is nearly twenty times per day. I don't know why and how I developed this habit—the origins of it. But now I am 'addicted' to water. Of course, this makes me use the bathroom more, but that is a small price to pay for good health.

Water being a zero-calorie drink, I don't put on weight because of this habit. My weight has remained the same in the last seven years—77 kg. In fact, my hydrating habit has helped me to reduce ten kilograms in the last four years. I am now overweight but not obese. I have a BMI of twenty-eight. Earlier it was forty. I can go without food for days, but I cannot stay without water for more than one hour. Additionally, I never go out without carrying water with me.

Water also detoxifies my body. Hangovers can be cured by drinking lots of water and nothing else. I also know that it prevents common problems like headaches and constipation. I urge the reader to drink water every hour of the day and judge for himself or herself. Drinking lots of water can be a cure-all for many common illnesses.

My other healthy habit (I don't have many) is getting at least eight hours of sleep. The emphasis here is that it must be night sleep and not during the daytime. Doctors recommend at least six to seven hours of night sleep. But personally, I need at least eight, which means that to get up early, I must ensure I am in bed by 10 p.m. I follow this to the letter, and I am happy with it. It has worked wonders for me.

Having been a journalist for most of my career, I had almost forgotten to sleep at night. I was forced to work until the wee hours of the morning and sleep after sunrise. This ruined my health, and I suffered from burnout. I don't want that to happen ever again.

Now, when I wake up, I am as lively as a lark. My mind is full of ideas, and I find that working early in the morning is better than later in the day. There are clever time management blogs that will tell you the same. More work and better-quality work gets done between 5.30 a.m. and breakfast time. It is an amazing time of the day.

Our sages called it *Brahma Muhurta*. This is when human consciousness is at its peak and vibing in sync with the universe. But all this is possible only if I get my quota of eight hours of sleep at night. When I don't get this much-needed sleep, I tend to be irritable, drowsy, and less effective the following day. It feels miserable.

Why Cry When I Die?

The question is not who will cry when I die, it is who laughs with me when I do. Life, as we know it matters, not death or the afterlife. We aren't ancient Egyptians—building giant pyramids to preserve our legacies. We leave behind happy families, profitable businesses, groundbreaking inventions in medicine and technology, and acclaimed works of art.

Perhaps, no one will cry when I die because I have not done anything remarkable. I am not even sure whether all the people I have crossed paths with still remember me. However, I am convinced I have led a meaningful life rich with varied experiences, lasting relationships, and some career achievements. I know gratification with gratitude.

If everyone can be great, then who is ordinary? It is ordinary people who validate the lives of great ones with their adoration, respect, and awe. It is okay for me to lead an ordinary life and go when my time comes if I have someone who loves and misses me when I am gone. That is the gist of it. One must lead a fulfilling life, not glorify the 'beyond'. This sounds radical but it must be so. However, everybody must wish and work towards dignity in death. Not suffering.

However, it is essential to lead an inspired life rather than an ordinary one. That is the only criterion needed to justify my existence. What inspires me is a question only I can answer.

Is it making money? Finding love? Helping people? Writing a book? Building the ultimate supercomputer? Finding a cure for Alzheimer's? Putting criminals behind bars? Defending my country? There are hundreds of lifepaths I can take to make life interesting, meaningful, and filled with a sense of achievement.

In my case, I determine the magnitude of achievement. I reserve the right to call it quits anytime I want. Or change lanes and do something different when I wish it. What I do needs to satisfy me and only me. That is what makes my life special to me.

It seldom matters to me if other people don't appreciate me when I am not 'working' for them. If they do, it's a bonus. When a life is thus lived, no one needs to regret that one has led an 'ordinary' life when the end is near. My life and work will always be special to me.

Fear of death intrigues me. In my fifty-plus years, there has not been a single moment when I feared death. Probably because I have been busy living. I have led a life rich with experiences and learning. It is quite possible that I am yet to face a situation where my very life is at stake. But as long as I am alive, death does not matter. Beyond that, nothing else matters because I feel no pain after death.

Section II

On People

Creating Win-Wins through Connection

I have an obsession, which isn't necessarily a bad one, but an obsession all the same. I like to connect people when I see synergies between the two parties. I do it out of goodwill, not for money or favours in return. I do it so that the two people I connect can gain something mutually. One has what the other lacks, so collaboration can turn into a win-win for both.

Having been a journalist for decades, I have made some contacts with people who are in a position to help others. They could be old colleagues, friends I went to college with or my own family. But whenever I meet someone who is need of something badly, my mind starts racing and I begin to visualise how someone I am close to can be of help in alleviating this person's problems.

Let me give you an example. A nephew who is pursuing a degree in social media marketing wants to intern at a social media management firm for a few months in order to fulfil his curriculum requirements. And it so happens that an old colleague and buddy is the co-founder and director of such an agency. Put two and two together, and you get a five, not four!

All I had to do was make some phone calls and forward my nephew's CV to my friend and the job got done. My nephew got his internship, and if he is quick to learn and hard-working during the internship, he is most likely to get his first career break at my friend's company as a digital media specialist.

I understand that my contribution to this whole happy episode was minimal. I just had to mediate. I am not the job-giver or the job-doer, I am someone who knows and cares for both parties. That does not make me an angel. It simply makes me a helpful person who is constantly mindful of how having connections and making use of them can help people in need.

I don't remember with clarity how many such instances have occurred in my life where I have connected people. Freshers got their first breaks, and others found the right specialist for their health complaints.

I have connected people to senior lawyers to put an end to protracted legal problems. Others have received scholarships and financial assistance to complete schooling, even believers seeking astrological consultation. Mind you, I haven't benefited from all this monetarily or in any other manner. Some people even say don't say a 'thank you', which is fine by me.

Why? Because I don't do it for money or praise. It is who I am. I get a high out of helping people in need. I am pretty sure there are several others who do it with kindness and selflessness. Who won't? It is just connecting people. However, in my case, it is an obsession. I like accumulating good karma. Nothing more. I am consciously, mindfully asking myself what good deed I can do for the day.

The Power of Working 'With' People

We have a lot of help around the house—from the driver to the cook, to the maid, gardener, and cleaner. As is the South Indian custom for addressing people in the plural to show respect, we extend this practice to all our house help. There is a clear reason why I do this. I want the house help to feel that they are working 'with' me, not 'for' me.

I have had a long tenure in journalism and the corporate world, and I have often wished that my bosses had the same attitude towards their subordinates. I have noticed that most bosses adopt a 'you-work-for-me' mindset simply because they are above others in the pay grade.

The problem with this kind of attitude is that it is condescending. The message it conveys is: 'I own your behind.' Therein lies the issue. Such an approach makes subordinates defensive rather than productive. When this happens, teams fall apart at the seams, and attrition increases.

Treating people with respect doesn't mean you have to go around calling everyone 'Sir' or 'Madam'. Respect is a fundamental ingredient in building cohesive and effective teams. With respect comes trust, and with trust and respect, teams begin to deliver stellar performances.

I firmly believe that paymasters should treat people with respect, kindness, and trust—regardless of their income level or educational background. The 'I pay you, so do as I say' attitude breeds contempt. Like all negative energies, this vibe weakens the team and reduces effectiveness.

Honestly, try this—it has worked for me when I led teams in Hyderabad and Bengaluru. Start by addressing your subordinates in the plural, with respect. Secondly, when time permits, engage in conversations about their families, especially their children's education, the health of elders, and other personal matters—without being intrusive.

You will probably spend just five minutes doing this, but the positivity it generates is immeasurable. This simple act brings the team member closer to you, fostering greater willingness to work for you. It cultivates loyalty—and with loyalty comes trust, respect, and effectiveness.

Although I have had few opportunities to lead teams—and only small ones, I know that I am an intuitive leader. One of my strengths, according to a Gallup Inc. test, is 'Individualisation'.

This means that my communication and interpersonal interactions are tailored to suit the person I am engaging with. No matter who I meet or interact with, my methods may change from one person to another, but one constant remains—respect. This is irrespective of the individual's socio-economic background.

Over the past thirty years, I can boldly claim that even when I did not value someone's work output, I have never treated them disrespectfully. In fact, I have often lowered my standards to accommodate the other person's preferences regarding food and other mundane matters.

However, the respect and affection that such individuals show in return outweigh any discomfort I might feel in those moments. These salt-of-the-earth people are often willing to go to great lengths to help me when I am in trouble—simply because they believe they 'work with me,' not 'for me.'

Threads of Community

People are often seen wearing company-given employee engagement T-shirts in public places like parks and malls. Why is that? Is it because they are proud of their company and want the world to know they work there? Or is there a deeper reason?

Pride is the obvious answer. But on reflection, one realises that what truly makes them wear these T-shirts is the sense of belonging they feel towards their company and co-workers. They want to be seen as part of something bigger—something that connects them existentially with others like them.

This 'need to belong to a larger whole' is a very real and compelling force that everyone feels throughout their lives—whether in a family or community gathering, attending elite club meetings, or participating in a demonstration for or against a cause.

The need to belong to a group is an innate longing that connects people and even shapes their identity. The point here is that people always seek similarities, not differences. And when they are different from those around them, they seek out others who are 'different' like them. It begins at birth and ends with death. Attachment to the smallest sociologically-proven unit—the family—is just the beginning.

How can you test this simple truth? Imagine you are marooned on an island with no other human beings around. In the absence of people, you begin to bond with trees and animals on the island. You may even make conversation with these mute companions to pass the time and stay sane until someone comes to rescue you. This is just the stuff of Hollywood movies, but it reflects reality.

The fact is that belongingness changes you, and your contribution to a community changes it. It works both ways. I have been part of several organisations over the last three decades, and each experience has changed me greatly. My contributions to these groups, however small, have left an impression on the people I interacted with. They remember me for 'something' I did when I was with them.

When I was young, I aspired to become a rock-climbing instructor because I was a member of an outward-bound club. Much later, I wanted to be a journalist because I became friendly with some. I worked in IT corporates because all my peers in college were making more money in IT. These groups shaped me just as I influenced them.

Much blood has been spilt in the name of religion. That is the downside of a sense of belonging. But choosing the right people to spend time with builds lasting bonds and enriches experiences. It's true that one is known by the company one keeps.

The Rare Gift of Genuine Friendship

The people you surround yourself with shape your personality. This means that you have to handpick your friends consciously. If you are the vivacious type who makes friends with almost anybody you meet, you run the risk of being disillusioned when they let you down. Fair-weather friends are a dime a dozen.

Good friends make life enjoyable. They are people who tolerate your idiosyncrasies, care for you, and make you laugh. They are willing to spend their time with you, which is saying a lot. I have certain yardsticks to define a true friend. The first question I ask myself when I grow close to someone is: 'Does this person make me feel comfortable?' It is as simple as that.

If my self-preservation instinct says yes, I grow closer to that person. This means that the person does not give rise to feelings of mistrust in me. I know their heart is true and they will do nothing to me that is not in my best interest.

The other is that the person I meet must not judge me. I detest having a friend who judges my every word and action. The very feeling of being judged makes me uncomfortable. I become wary and defensive as opposed to open and honest.

People who judge me cynically can never be my friends because, by the very act of judging me, they are trying to establish superiority. I make friends among equals, not narcissists. This explains why I don't have too many friends in high places—although most of my friends are people who set very high standards for themselves.

I want to make friends that I can look up to—people who inspire me towards achievement. Take, for example, two of my college friends who never abandoned me in the last thirty years. They work hard, earn, save, travel, read widely, think pragmatically, maintain excellent health, and are devoted to their families. They are ethical. They are leaders in their chosen vocations. Just being with them makes me a better person. I cherish, admire, and stick to friends like that, as, in their company, I am the best I can be.

Another quality I look for in a friend is honesty—not transactional, but absolute. I will never trust a person who lies to me. If there is no trust, there is no friendship. A dishonest individual is like a snake in the grass. I have known such people. They win your trust and then take advantage of you, leaving you betrayed. They come into your life with malintent and disappear when you need them.

Finally, I want to be forgiven by my friends for the wrong I unwittingly did to them. A forgiving friend is the best there is. My friend should have the broadmindedness to let go of the past and remain in my circle.

I want friends for life; not someone who leaves no impression or memory of having met. I was looking at a class of 1987 picture taken when I was in school and realised that among the fifty faces there, I could recognise only one—my school bestie. He revived contact with me after forty years, which means that all the others in the photograph are of no consequence.

Why We Stay, Why We Go

This is the menacing question that all of us are faced with more often than necessary in life. When will you say, 'Thus far and no further'? Unless there is a prophet willing to part the sea for your safe passage, you must decide for yourself. I have asked this question many times. Suffering is necessary, it builds character. But enduring lifelong misery is meaningless.

Life can turn into a never-ending loop, and you find yourself suffering without reason. You feel as though you have no choice. In the eastern part of the world, people often attribute this to fate. They feel powerless, hopeless, and worthless. They descend into depression and lifelong agony begins there.

There is a reason why I penned this article. It has nothing to do with my problems, failures, or disappointments. But I have known at least half a dozen couples unhappy with their marriages.

The same applies to overprotective parents, siblings, and children who endure abuse day after day without respite. Dysfunctional families are common, as are dysfunctional teams.

However, it takes great courage to say—thus far and no further. To break away from a relationship and choose happiness, particularly when you are not the cause of the unhappiness and have fulfilled all that is expected of you as a family member or colleague.

I have been in dysfunctional relationships. I have often suffered more than the other person. Yet, I have never had the courage to end the relationship. Luckily for me, the relationship was always ended by the other party. Perhaps they were wiser than I—more practical, if nothing else. I know at least three people who walked away from me.

But I have noticed one indisputable fact. The person who causes pain in a demeaning relationship often dies or leaves long before the victim. The abuser's karma catches up with them sooner rather than later.

It is not due to a significant age gap between the two. It is simply the way it happens. The universe grants those who have known prolonged suffering some respite in their later years—often even happiness. This truth offers a glimmer of hope to those trapped in abusive relationships.

So why don't people just walk away from such torment? I have known such individuals, and they share two sterling qualities—love and hope. They are incredibly loving and incurably optimistic.

In my book, they are godly, not human. They continue to forgive and adjust until the end. In some cases, their patience is rewarded by a change in circumstances that brings them happiness. In others, the abuser simply gets paid in the same coin and dies a miserable death.

Karma is ubiquitous and infallible, you see.

The Problem with 'Nice'

I wonder what people actually mean when they say 'nice'. Does it mean something is good, mediocre, or bad? 'Nice' is perhaps the most misused and misunderstood word in English. When I really bother to think about it, I find that people who say I am nice, or that my article is nice, are being condescending. They say 'nice' because they cannot. or do not want to. express their displeasure more explicitly.

I am not ungrateful to people who take the time to read my articles and express their appreciation. I am lucky to have such friends and family. But 'nice'? Why not 'intriguing'? 'Thought-provoking'? Or some other specific and meaningful praise? Is it that they are unwilling to express their appreciation but do so anyway out of pity?

Without becoming paranoid and letting my hyperactive imagination run wild, I admit that not everyone has a gift for language. Perhaps in their vocabulary, 'nice' really means 'good' or 'splendid'. However, I find that those who do take the trouble to respond to my work with appreciation are mostly well-read and highly intelligent. They do have literary prowess. It would really help if people were more specific.

To me, 'nice' is patronising feedback. People say 'nice' because they want to be 'nice' to me and avoid hurting my feelings. After all, every writer thinks they are gifted, and the work they produce means the world to them. When someone comments that the work is lacking in some way, the writer is hurt. This is generally understood by most. So, when people say 'nice', they are showing concern, not appreciation. And for that I am thankful.

I find that even 'fine' is better than 'nice'. I understand that people don't have the time to weigh the connotations of different words before reacting to consider how their feedback will be perceived. Their lives are too busy for such trivialities. But my request is this—when you judge me or my work, please elaborate a little. That way, I have an opportunity to improve myself.

If something in my article is good, please let me know why you think so. If something is amiss, let me know what is wrong. I am the kind of writer who takes feedback very seriously, especially if I value the judgement of the person giving it.

Saying 'nice' is so vague that it confuses me. It is useless to me. If you take the trouble to read my work and respond, please take just one more minute to tell me why you think the article is 'nice'. This makes your feedback valuable to me, and, in my mind, you become a VIP.

Better still, share my article with someone else. That way, I gain more readers—and more readers mean more feedback. In turn, this means more opportunities to improve myself and my work. Next time you show appreciation, not just to me but to anyone else who has done a good job, please be articulate. You have no idea how happy that makes the writer or the doer of the job. For you, it is just fifteen seconds. For someone like me, it brings sheer joy.

The Two Faces of Success: Creativity and Smartness

All through history, breakthroughs in science, technology, art, and literature have come about due to the work of creative and imaginative people. Not smart ones. Smart people are a dime a dozen. But it is the creative people endowed with vivid imagination who have thought differently and created lasting works of art and inventions that make the world a better place. Creativity and smartness are not mutually exclusive. They often manifest in the same person.

Creativity and imagination are the roots. Creative people often wonder, '*What if . . . ?*' and then embark on the road to invention or discovery. Smart people are the branches that spread out, yield, and ripen the fruit. They put great ideas to work. All my life, people have deemed me a creative person. Many of them are also aware of how easily I can be outsmarted. While creativity is my gift, smartness is something I have yet to receive.

Consider this: Leonardo Da Vinci was both an artist and an inventor. The faculties of his mind that he used to create his paintings and inventions were a product of his creativity and imagination, not his smartness. Similarly, a creative person invented the coffee maker, blender, and toaster. But the businessperson who monetised the idea, made millions of them, and sold them for a profit was 'smart'. I admire people with seminal ideas—both creative and smart.

Einstein's 'Theory of Relativity' was an extremely abstract and pivotal idea that resulted from his creative and imaginative mind. His curiosity compelled him to seek beyond the 'Newtonian' obvious. But the atomic bomb was made and used by smart scientists and politicians to end a devastating war.

This also proves that a single inventor like Thomas Edison can invent many things, while it takes millions of smart people in the lighting solutions industry to make money out of the electric bulb and its variants for generations.

Edison was a single prolific scientist driven by the innate need to invent. But his invention feeds millions of smart people's families via their jobs. They may not thank him at every meal, but needless to say, they are grateful for the job, which, again, is an outcome of Edison's ingenuity. Being a creative and imaginative person responsible for many of life's greatest comforts is a great distinction indeed.

Creativity, imagination, and smartness. What is really required, I wonder. Simply put, each generation needs its creative and imaginative people to make lives better as life becomes more harried and complex. Without these gems, humanity would not have progressed beyond the invention of the wheel. I ask myself if I can survive a single day without using the internet and I have my answer.

What then of smart people? Well, they are indispensable. They turn the wheels of industry that make an astounding invention a household appliance. The quality of their thinking is in no way inferior to that of the creative person.

They are smart because they 'see' value in the invention. Without them, the invention has no real value—monetarily or in terms of utility. It could get lost among the hundreds of inventions that never saw the light of day in this competitive world where there is an upgrade every few weeks. They are the people who sponsor and empower geniuses. The genius can afford to be naïve in business matters and leave the task of bringing inventions into the real world to smart people.

Without smart people, entire economies and their ecosystems—like families—would starve to death or die without cures for sickness. It is smart people who design the vehicles that allow consumers to derive the benefit of the inventions of creative and imaginative people.

I imagine a society without money, where I find it exasperating to barter with my cow for some medicine that a sick, dying child needs. Is my cow too little an exchange for medication? Or too much? How do I convert my cow into medicine? After centuries since the invention of money and a banking system, I don't need to struggle with such banal dilemmas. Thanks to the 'smart' people who 'invented' money.

The Wounds of Pride and Intelligence

There are two situations that make people angry—when others' remarks or actions hurt their pride, or when their intelligence is insulted. I belong to the category where I take offence in both these situations. When someone hurts my pride, I get angry. But when someone insults my intelligence, I am livid.

It is not about being hypersensitive to criticism. Criticism is always good in any situation. Without other people doing our black hat thinking for us, we never evolve as individuals, organisations, or even as humans. People who question my motives, logic, and work are a godsend. They are my friends in disguise, I reckon. Critics must be regarded highly in all societies as long as they are experts on what they are criticising. Without people poking holes in our theories, we stop getting better over time. Our personal or business growth comes to stasis. And then the rot sets in. This is the beginning of the end.

What I am opposed to is people hurting my pride with below-the-belt attacks. Such attacks are personal, carefully targeted to lower a person's esteem, self-image, and public image. These attacks are intentional, not arbitrary. Such jeers damage reputations and undervalue the person's worth.

The values of people who get a kick out of insulting others are questionable. Considering that most snide attacks—verbal or otherwise—are made by people who have no pride or are not intelligent, it makes one wonder whether they do it out of jealousy.

Jealousy is a highly intense emotion. It drives people to commit heinous crimes. This is a well-established fact. Could the same emotion make people strike out at those they envy? Does that mean that the attacker feels lacking in something that their target has in abundance? Could that be the attacked person's pride and intelligence? I once had a boss who told me that if people are jealous of me, that is a sign that I am doing the job well. Her words turned out to be true.

Without making the fatal error of overestimating my sense of self-worth, should I take such insults and use them to fuel my ambitions? Or must I feel hurt and complain about being victimised? I wonder.

But negative emotions like jealousy are highly capable of draining positive energy. Casting out the 'evil eye' can leave a person exhausted. Instead of using my energy to create something beautiful that helps others, too, I waste my energy fighting people who have nothing else to do other than hurt people they envy. This is a pointless battle, and nobody really wins this. Definitely not me.

The only logical way out is to ignore such people and move on. Who knows what great things I might achieve going forward? I must conserve my energy for them to manifest, not take on small-minded people who have no pride or intelligence.

The Perils of Knowing It All

I have no problem with people sticking to their own opinions. It's a free country, and they have every right to do so. Dissent is the voice of progress and the very foundation of democracy—whether in a country, society, or organisation.

People, by nature, are unique. No one is exactly like the other in every single way—not even twins. This is why they are called 'individuals'. Their ideas, beliefs, values, and biases are all 'individualistic'. Several like-minded people can indeed come together and move mountains—create miracles. But even then, there are bound to be disagreements on how to move the mountain.

What irks me are people who have an opinion on everything. I have come across many such people—gurus, self-styled 'omnipotent' generalists, journalists, writers, politicians, singers, actors, film-makers, cricketers, and so on. Many of these professions have little foundation in scientific knowledge and practice. That is not a coincidence.

Rarely does one find a rocket scientist, doctor, or engineer publicly commenting on matters beyond their scope of understanding—unless, they have political ambitions.

Why? Because 'science-driven people' base all their opinions on expertise or specialisation—their science. It is pertinent for them to seek scientific or empirical evidence.

Lawyers and teachers, however, straddle both realms—scientific and unscientific. This is why they often make popular politicians. They enjoy the best of both worlds.

Scientists, doctors, and engineers recognise the limits of their understanding and strive to seek greater knowledge in areas they cannot objectively evaluate. They often turn to experts in the relevant field. They are curious to know others' opinions on issues they are not familiar with. They are honest and sincere. Politicians, however, feel compelled to make statements about all things—relevant and irrelevant.

To be fair, this book covers a wide range of topics. It is up to you to keep reading—or punish me, a journalist, for having an opinion on many things. The difference is that I am sincere. So please, keep reading. I admit my imperfections.

Consider this bizarre scenario: The Earth is about to be invaded by aliens. Politicians and ordinary citizens are all over your TV and social media feeds, making statements—even when they have very little time to live. All for their fifteen seconds of fame. If a scientist appears on TV, it's likely because they have no political ambitions.

The real people gearing up for the attack are totally focused on saving the planet. They have no time to speak to the media. It is these people who believe in the power of science, technology, and mathematics that make the difference.

They are the treasures of modern society. They need to be protected, encouraged, and supported. The glamour pages of newspapers will always exist. But what do you read first—the front page or the gossip column? Your choice reveals the kind of person you are—serious or frivolous.

People who have opinions on everything often have a personal agenda. Disprove this, and I'll happily accept your opinion on anything. It's not a crime to have an opinion on everything—so long as I keep it private. But if I choose to make my opinions public, I must ask myself: How much do I really know about the topic?

Vague vs Specific People

I have noticed that people are usually one of two things when they share information—vague or specific. I believe that people who are vague are unsure of themselves or wish to hide pertinent information. Conversely, people who are specific are more often than not truthful in their interactions. They are people with integrity. They are authentic.

Vague people are those who don't believe in what they say. They don't have real answers. They respond to questions with more inconclusive questions. Here's an example: I asked an old friend, who reconnected with me voluntarily after decades, a simple question that one asks an old bestie, 'How many children do you have?'

His reply was unthinkable, 'Cheaper by the dozen!'

This text message was enough for me to conclude that I must stop asking further questions about the state of his marriage or children—if he even has sired any. My question was harmless. An ordinary one. But it clearly pushed all the wrong buttons. Since then, I have no idea about his marriage and have not bothered to probe beyond the vague answer to my innocuous query.

However, experience tells me that when someone answers my question specifically, they are well-informed and honest, if nothing else. Specific people have little to hide. They make eye contact when they speak. They pride themselves on knowing things that I don't. They may even talk down to me, which is fine, because they know more than I do.

Vague people, on the other hand, are avoidant—not just in answering questions posed to them but also in other interactions. They do not make eye contact. They use crude humour to disguise their dubious answers or statements. They are eccentric and irritating at times. An average person might ignore them and their opinions, but for me, they are a subject of study.

So how does one decide whether a person is being vague or specific? Simple conscious reasoning will provide the answer in less than five minutes of face-to-face interaction or over the phone. The trick is to identify whether the person comes across as an 'artful dodger'. (What the Dickens!) If your subject is one, they will give a vague answer to at least three consecutive simple questions.

Additionally, they will use crude humour—a dead giveaway. For instance, if someone is drunk-texting you and you reply asking whether they are drinking, they are likely to respond with something like: 'Life is short. Make it sweet.'

By contrast, an authentic and specific person might reply: 'Why are you asking me this question? I am stone-cold sober! I want you to tell me why that question came to your mind?' Such a specific person is likely to take great offense with you considering them drunk at work.

As a rule, vague people are less impactful in any life situation. They don't matter. Their eccentricity does not guarantee intelligence or usefulness, although highly eccentric people are often very intelligent. They are artful dodgers. People who mean business don't dodge difficult questions.

Living Alone, Living Well

I know people who are essentially single and live alone. However, they don't feel lonely. This is a laudable quality to have. In another place in this book, I have stated that to be is to belong and that people always need to experience a sense of belonging. This is absolutely true.

Those who live alone and do not feel lonely are the exceptions to this rule. They are incredibly unique and possess fine qualities that can be emulated by those who often feel lonely. They are self-reliant and get all their daily chores done themselves.

I reckon, for all that they cannot or do not want to do, they would have saved up enough money to hire help. Someone once asked one such person, 'Don't you feel bored?'

She replied, 'I don't have the time to.' She was busy throughout the day editing math textbooks for a publisher. That is what I call a quip.

Considering that man is a social animal (Aristotle said it first), it follows that people who live alone and do not feel lonely must have strategies—hate to call them defence mechanisms—that allow them to be so.

Firstly, they maintain rigid routines. They are sticklers for structure. With dogged determination, they do the same things at the same time each day. This helps them remain fearless and strong. Secondly, they are careful with their money and health, a trait common among those who live alone.

Being away from other people most of the time is challenging. It takes a special kind of mettle. It means you have to plan and ensure that you have enough resources—material and spiritual—to keep you sane and functional.

I read an article where the researchers claim that more people die of loneliness than those who smoke (Pantell et al. 2013). A recent study posted on the internet shows that loneliness is as dangerous as smoking fifteen cigarettes a day.

Being alone can drive a person crazy. It means that you are fighting an innate desire to be among people. You are going against the grain, nature itself. It requires tremendous courage and determination.

I find that the people in question here have plenty of it. They have meticulously envisaged a life of solitude, silence, self-reliance, frugality, and acceptance. They are cautious to take good care of their health because they know that when illness occurs, they have no one to rush to their bedside and take care of them. They make every effort possible to remain motivated and mobile even in advanced age. They know they cannot afford to lose their independence.

Such people may sometimes come across as selfish. In my opinion, this is not true. There are several lonely people who generously donate to lost causes without seeking publicity for it. The stereotype of an old, lonely Scrooge is merely a cliché. In fact, one such person I know donates to save homeless dogs.

I have also noticed that people who live alone do not invest in property and luxury items. They are more likely to spend large amounts of money on solo travel. There is a reason for this: Why invest in fixed assets when you have no one to leave it to when you go? Being an alone person does not mean you have to lead a boring and staid life. It means that you are in a unique position to do what you want with your life and money because your actions do not impact anyone else.

What way to live!

Mastering the Process Trio

I believe three kinds of processes are essential for the success of any project: Entertaining ideas, putting them to work, measuring progress, and making improvements. Any task needs people with vision, people who execute them, and quality analysts. All other roles are supportive and derivative.

But when one is self-employed or leading a small team, one needs to be all three kinds of people rolled into one. In my career, I have been all three people. As a freelancer, I am now a one-man enterprise.

I ideate, create, refine, and deliver. When the process of envisioning happens, I ask the question, '*What if?*' I have standard execution processes, and I measure the output and make it better. Understanding this universal principle and applying it to personal development could be helpful. I play all three roles because I cannot afford to hire a team.

To achieve my vision, I need to ask myself what I want, match that with what I am capable of achieving, and where I should seek help. To be an executor, I need a plan of action to improve the quality and velocity of decision-making and be result-oriented. To measure what is done, I need to periodically review my work and devise solutions to detriments.

For instance, this book was a wild idea that popped up in my mind when I was writing columns for a local newspaper. At first, it seemed impossible. Then I let the thought marinate for a few days. But even before penning the first essay, I had to know more about the publishing industry. So, I called a friend who had authored and published three books, and she gave me many valuable insights.

The idea in my mind began to take shape and I could see with my mind's eye that I could become a writer of some significance. The key here is that I saw the book as complete, successful, and best-selling. I began to weave daydreams of people appreciating my work. These fantasies were important for me to take the first few steps, like cold mailing my publisher some samples of my work. Game on.

Then came the arduous execution stage. I began to write prolifically. I set up a weekly writing routine. Facing a three-month deadline, I was compelled to think and act fast. I had to use all my creativity, stamina, and willpower to avoid procrastination—which is one of my many failings.

I had to write a minimum of one essay each day whether I was inspired or not. I could not afford a 'writer's block'. But as time passed, this was no longer an impediment. I felt inspired all the time. I would immediately note down a new idea and write on it that very day. I made a laundry list of ideas in my scrapbook and now I find that I have put almost 90 per cent of all the ideas to work.

Finally, review. At the end of each essay, I had to proofread the copy and make it more readable and precise. I wrote over 100 essays, but I had to weed out a dozen or so because they didn't align with the theme of this book.

I had to keep track of the word count because I had a 50,000-word target. I would often go back to the chapters that I had written weeks earlier to read the article with a different frame of mind—to check whether it made sense or not. Or if it was in bad taste. All this was a lot of work. But if you are reading this, I trust that it was all worth it.

Observation— A Quiet Advantage

When I was young, I saw a poster of a leopard cub staring at the horizon, with the quote below it reading: 'You observe a lot by watching.' In hindsight, I realise how true this statement is. Even as toddlers, we learn by watching our caregivers, much like a leopard cub learns to hunt by observing the elders in its pride.

As we grow up, we continue this process. As trainees, we shadow subject matter experts to learn the processes of the business. This has become a lifelong pursuit for me. I observe people to learn how best I can optimise my time. I assimilate what I need and discard what is not suitable.

Observing people and wondering what makes them tick is a pastime I inherited from my mother, who used to attend weddings and gatherings only to sit quietly in a corner, watching people. She often told me she enjoyed it for the sheer pleasure of guessing what each person's agenda was for attending the gathering.

It is worth noting that my mother had strong likes and dislikes and could be opinionated. But observing people was her way of passing time 'constructively' at large gatherings, where everyone seemed busy and important. She was not always right in her assessments, but she was reasonably accurate most of the time. Her evaluations of people often proved correct in the long run.

Watching people has its advantages. When I watch, I begin to observe patterns of behaviour, providing me with crude data about a person's outer and inner self.

My instincts for self-preservation—fight, flight, or freeze—passed down from countless ancestors, trigger a train of thought about an individual's behaviour. I don't need to be a transactional analyst to deduce—from their words and body language—whether someone is an introvert, extrovert, or ambivert. This process begins naturally and continues until I gather enough information to decide whether an interaction with them will be pleasant and beneficial or otherwise.

Of course, my conclusions are not always foolproof. There may be many gaps in my final reckoning. However, keeping an open mind and avoiding distraction from preconceived notions allows me to make better assessments. If I can set aside bias, I discover how useful this seemingly innocuous pastime can be. Observing others often reveals truths that are, later, confirmed when I interact with them and validate my gut feelings.

It's not just people you come to understand by watching—it's also events. Correlating prior experiences with current situations helps identify patterns in occurrences. This can guide decisions about whether to stay or leave an event. However, to gain such insights, one must first observe carefully and mentally take notes.

Next time you are at a gathering, consciously watch and observe. You might be surprised at how much better you understand both people and events.

The Gift of Insight

I see everything. But I don't usually talk about it. Noticing everything is my curse. I am not sure why I have this ability, but I have been this way since childhood. I see things that other people simply don't pay attention to, and I even go as far as analysing them. But nine times out of ten, I keep my trap shut and don't comment on what I have observed.

If you are wondering what the heck I am talking about, let me give you an example. I notice your eyebrow going up a notch when we are conversing. This is hypothetical, but that is the level of detail my brain records—for later analysis—during the conversation. The raising of the eyebrow and your body language intrigues me, especially if you are a new acquaintance. It can even be as remote and impersonal for old friends and family as a text message.

I see and save every facial muscle twitch, voice intonation, and eye movement when I interact with people directly or indirectly (like in an online meeting). I have the ability to make sense of that one-second emotion. This is not bragging. It is true.

One thing I am gifted with is a good memory. I forget what I had for breakfast, but I remember instances from my kindergarten days. My long-term memory—like most ageing people's; nothing new there—is far better than my short-term memory. Cut to the present. I am fifty-three. I have a lot of life and work experience. As a reporter, I have crossed paths with many kinds of people—from politicians to criminals to famous sportspeople to film stars to religious influencers. I am a seventies-born individual. I have seen everything from the advent of the personal computer to AI/ML. Considering that the world is changing every few weeks, I have the best of many worlds.

However, if you are inquisitive, you might want to know how I do it—gleaning things about people. To begin with, I have frames of reference. I remember people not by their public image, but by their interactions with me. I try to understand their idiosyncrasies—things that are unique to them or people like them. Most often, I can sense when a person is lying or faking it. But I let it pass. Why? Well, no one is perfect.

I know I am not! Then I try and understand—through some secondary research on the internet—who they are, what they do, their origins, achievements, and debacles, if any. I profile them as a pastime. If I know their origin, their current position in society, and what they do and say, I have most of what I need to process this subject.

Given all this, one needs to be as observant as me to get the final set of data needed for the analysis. Meet the person and look for 'out-of-place' reactions—anomalies. Inconsistencies. I am spending nearly an hour authoring this essay, but the process of recognition takes only a fraction of a minute for me. As time passes and I get to spend more time with the person, I start filing away additional information about the personality with relative ease.

Figuring out what makes people tick is an obsession I have. I was probably born that way. I do it each time I meet someone known or unknown. It is a kind of reflex action. After years of therapy for paranoid schizophrenia, I now realise that my curse is a gift.

Finding Freedom in Frameworks

Each of us is given twenty-four hours a day. How we use it is defined by structure. 'Structure' refers to your daily routine. How you structure time is debatable, but the real question is: What connection does structure have with sanity? Life can throttle even the most hardened soul—those who usually face hardship with equanimity and manage to cope, if not overcome, trying situations.

A closer look at the lives of certain people reveals a startling relationship between their rigid, uncompromising dedication to routine and their fortitude in adversity. There are octogenarians in my family who take a morning walk 365 days a year—come rain or shine. Others play tennis daily at the age of eighty-five without missing a single day.

When I see such people, I envy them for their determination. It makes them seem superhuman. Yet for them, their walks and tennis matches are rote. Their temperament is something to aspire to. They have pleasing demeanours and remain surprisingly calm in testing times. I never cease to wonder how they maintain their composure and stability, even when facing bereavement.

There are also family elders who immerse themselves in religious rituals and spiritual practices for most of the day, performing them with utmost faith and precision. They, too, are surprisingly balanced and cheerful. They lead simple lives, but they are not simpletons. These are people endowed with significant intellectual capability.

But what about structure and sanity? My proposition is that there is a definite link. Maintaining sanity has a great deal to do with predictability and stability. A 'normal' person is often predictable, doing the same things at the same time daily. Such self-discipline is enviable, and adherence to routine seems to make these people mentally stable, even strong.

This may be because when they are involved in their routines, they do not dwell on the 'rest' of their lives. Even the multitudes who go to work daily often worry less about life's problems while they are at work. This is a common experience.

For those who believe that 'normal' is boring, here is a question: What is wrong with being a creature of habit? Habits maketh man. Everyone structures time uniquely, irrespective of how they are judged. Ultimately, I am the best judge of my behaviour. A little introspection is warranted.

My perspective is that when habits are empowering, they should be reinforced each day. In my observation, people with empowering structures are self-driven, dependable, and live with purpose. A habit that makes me powerless is bad for me. It is really that simple.

The Art of Thoughtful Generosity

When life treats me kindly—when I get everything I wish for in a situation, and the universe is generous to me in more ways than one—what should I do? Should I soak up every bit of it and stash away some comforts for an uncertain future? Or should I pass it on? Just a little—something I can afford to part with forever?

As a schoolchild, I read an article in *Reader's Digest*, which my father subscribed to. That's when I first understood the meaning of 'passing it on'. It means that when I experience some kind of windfall—be it money, recognition, gadgets, or otherwise—and I find myself with more than I need, I share those gifts with someone less fortunate.

For as long as I can remember, I have been this way. There have been times when I imposed my will on others, 'helping' them even when they hadn't asked for assistance.

Being born in October, I have a fixation on fairness. It unsettles me to see others deprived of things I possess. In my mind, this feels unjust. And so, I perform my 'helpful Hannah' act—even when those close to me advise against it, warning that I might find myself in need one day if I squander my good fortune.

I sometimes wonder if offering help to those who haven't asked for it is a step too far. What drives me to do this? Am I seeking an ego boost by assisting others without checking if they actually need my help? Is it simply because *I* want to feel good?

There is nothing wrong with feeling uplifted by helping others. However, when I impose myself on people, it eventually leads to unintended consequences. Instead of gratitude, my helpfulness can drive them away. They may begin to view me as intrusive rather than angelic.

Over time, they may avoid me, fail to return my calls, and stop offering praise. When that happens, the euphoria fades—I find myself lamenting their ingratitude, even though the fault lies entirely with me.

To truly pass it on, I must first ensure that the people I aim to help *want* my assistance. Secondly, I need to consider if they are genuinely deserving. Most importantly, I must reflect on whether I can realistically afford to help—and if so, to what extent.

There is a downside to helping others—it can make them dependent. Before taking action, I need to assess whether this is likely in their case. If my help inadvertently disempowers them and fosters reliance, I am not truly helping. Instead, I risk adding to their struggles—and my own.

Promises: Broken and Kept

Hark! What you say does not matter; what you do does. People often say things thoughtlessly. Many even make promises when they realise they cannot keep them. This is sheer dishonesty.

Promises are made and broken every day. A broken promise belittles both the one who promises and the one who suffers because of it. It erodes trust and respect for the person who made the promise and creates resentment in the person who is betrayed. But deeds are remembered for a long time, not just by the doer, but also by the people they are done to. Especially the good ones. Action is a confirmation of the commitment. Words are just fluff.

Take a common example. Someone you know dies, and you find out. A majority of people find it enough to text the bereaved family an 'RIP' message with some shallow condolences. But if the deceased has been a kind, benevolent soul, a person who has received a favour or two from them, will attend their funeral. The same goes for birthday parties and weddings. The others are superficial.

Or take another common example. You are between jobs and flat broke. The friend who lends you money is not really doing you a favour. They are making you dependent. A friend who proactively finds you a position in their company is a true pal. They are empowering you to fend for yourself.

I have made many, many promises that I have failed to keep. But whenever I fail to keep my word, it bugs me. Perhaps I have an overactive conscience. But it certainly pains me not to keep my word. I become anxious and troubled when I have failed to keep my word. Especially when the other person is in trouble and genuinely needs help.

I have also come across many people whose words I can take for granted. They are people I respect and trust. Even if they delay or fail to keep their word, I don't mind. Because I know I can depend on them at another time. They are solid. There are others with whom I deal with carefully. Because they over-promise and under-deliver. But they, too, are not on my toxic people list. Especially when they are fighting their own battles and do not have the time or the resources to help me. I understand this intuitively and am willing to wait or waive.

However, certain people are as shallow as the promises they make. These are my 'avoid-this-toxic-person' type. Interestingly, when such a person makes me a promise or asks for my help, I am convinced that their intentions are foul. This person is not to be trusted at all, and with this type, I ask for no quarter, nor give any. Over the years, I have been short-changed so many times that now I have developed a radar sense that triggers blaring alarms in my mind when I come across such a person.

To conclude, what is said is irrelevant. It is meaningful only in hindsight. Action taken, or even an honest willingness to do so, is the proof of the pudding. When a given word is not backed by action, it is empty and leaves behind shattered hopes, resentment, and feelings of betrayal. This is why I don't make empty promises. If someone asks for my help and I realise I am incapable of delivering, I tell them the honest reason why my hands are tied and ask to be excused.

The Large-Heartedness of Animal Lovers

I have made one observation. People who are kind to animals are generally large-hearted. They are tolerant, patient, kind, and generous. I am in awe of people who rescue animals when natural and manmade disasters strike. It takes a special kind of heart to do this—one that beats for all things living.

I am not talking particularly about animal welfare activists. I am referring to kind, ordinary people who have pets at home and care to feed homeless dogs. If you look a bit closely, such people are respectful and generally broadminded in their dealings with other people. They try to understand your point of view and if they are close to you, they are quick to lend support when needed. Compassion is endemic to them and manifests in all their relations.

I have also noticed that animal lovers have a fetish for fairness. They believe that animals should be treated like humans and not as lesser beings. It is common for such people to consider and refer to their dogs and cats as a part of the family. They care for their pets while they are sick just as one would look after a sick child or ageing mother. The question is why?

I think that people who like animals have a fundamental respect for all of nature. They treat others the way they expect to be treated—well. Even the non-vegetarians among them find opportunities to have pets at home. But one finds that true animal-loving people are all vegetarians. Their case against animal killing—and for veganism—is a water-tight credo.

Their love for nature's children spills over to people as well. Animal-loving people are mostly reasonable and amenable. When they get into arguments they try to put themselves in the other man's shoes and walk a mile. They are empathetic and resourceful.

They make good team players. They are less egocentric than most. They make good parents, relatives, and friends. They are lively in the way they express their love and enjoy being with people. They are genuinely friendly and seldom complain about other people's idiosyncrasies. They are more accepting and have many friends.

I've noticed that narrow-minded people often do not have pets or care for animals. However, this doesn't imply that everyone without pets is narrow-minded. Perish the thought! But such people are usually self-centred.

They consider animals 'unclean'. Their veganism is more religious than a choice. They care only about themselves and their families. They consider those with pets foolish and naïve. It would be appropriate to mention here that we have three dogs at home. We call them the 'little ones'.

Paw parents make the world a better place to live in because of their capacity to care deeply. Thank god for small mercies!

The Joy of Simple Folk

I have noticed that I am better with grassroots people than with celebrities. As a news reporter, I have met all kinds of people—kings, queens of stardom, and plebs. But the stories that I wrote about popular people were of no consequence.

The stories I wrote about ordinary people came from the heart, not the head. This does not make me a potential electoral candidate. I detest politics. But it makes me more humane than many other people. I find that my interactions with grassroots people—the house help, cook, driver, cleaner, and gardener are more meaningful to me than some celebrities I interviewed a long time ago.

I have noticed that grassroots people are genial, kind, sincere, and highly empathetic. If they like me, they go all the way to be helpful and supportive without seeking anything in return other than respect. They are not vain and selfish like popular and influential people . . . or those with means. It is easier to trust them than to trust affluent and so-called educated people.

I remember my graduate college days. My roommates and I used to go to the house of a roadside hotel owner called Basappa for dinner each day. We used to pay him Rs 300 a month for dinner. Basappa never went to school and was illiterate.

Our daily visit to his thatch-roofed house was such a big deal for Basappa that he used to lavish us with a different sweet for dinner every day. He used to serve us ragi balls and lentil soup daily and top it up with some rural delicacy each night.

I doubt he made his money from us. For him, four educated youths coming home for dinner each day was a joyful experience. He would quiz us on politics, sports, sandalwood, and college life in general. His enthusiasm was infectious, and he made it his mission to entertain us with his stories of rustic life in his village as a youngster before he migrated to Mysore to set up his tea stall.

I recalled the Basappa experience to illustrate how warm and dependable grassroots people are. Almost without exception, the people who live in villages and small towns are large-hearted—they consider it a privilege to entertain strangers at home.

I realised this recently when I visited a small town, Shahpur, in my state for a survey. I was meeting these people for the first time, and they were meeting me for the first time as well. However, a lady who was responsible for our hospitality ensured that we were served delicious tea, lunch, and dinner promptly. She made me feel like royalty.

Grassroots people are true-hearted. They are seldom cunning or have ulterior motives. If they want something from you, they simply ask for it humbly. They do not pretend. I find that grassroots people are more mature than city people because they are accepting of the fact that they don't know much about anything. All that they know are things that educated and well-to-do people tell them. My heart goes out to such people, and I will always treat them with the respect they so richly deserve.

Lessons from the Young

Gary Zukav, in his record-selling book, *The Dancing Wu Li Masters*, says that a 'master' is simply someone who started before you did. However, in the internet age, a master can be younger, less experienced, and more aware and insightful than you. The awareness quotient of woke, young people today is far greater than my entire learning of fifty-three years.

They are born into an age of information anxiety and struggle to keep pace with trends daily. They simply gorge on all things on social media, however shallow or irrelevant the information is, but they are better clued in than most people my age.

I had the opportunity to learn from people 20–25 years younger than me when I was teaching full-time as a professor of journalism and mass communication at a college. I have gladly received and followed their sagacious advice on plenty of things—from how to use WhatsApp to what not to post on Facebook. These are things that my young students learn from each other long before their parents gift them their first smartphone.

In my day, there were only four essential survival skills to learn—how to cook, drive, type, and swim. Today, you need to be able to code in a dozen languages, master soft skills, learn how to prompt and use AI, and know how to utilise digital media to build your brand. Without these basic and several other necessary skills, you are headed nowhere. People today don't believe in destiny and luck—they make their own.

When I was young, all my masters were much older than I was. They had what could be loosely termed 'life experience' and some knowledge of their chosen line of work. But being older was a prerequisite in all of them. I would never take a person younger than me or of my age group seriously.

I remember my days as a university student. Most of the textbooks and notes were in English. While studying in groups, I would translate the gist of the notes to my Kannada-speaking mates, and I must admit that it helped me a great deal. The dual act of reading in English and translating it orally made the retention doubly effective. Needless to say, I topped the university in the exams.

Now I am trumped in any argument with teenagers. They are more knowledgeable than I am and certainly more intuitive. They have loads of experience in real life because they travel and read more at a remarkably young age.

They quickly adapt to rapid changes. But certainly, without exception, they are sure of what they want out of life. They have plans and persevere to achieve goals. I am learning from these twenty-somethings now—they are my new masters.

Being dismissive of young people is the biggest mistake that one can make as a teacher or mentor. It would be better to first ascertain how much they know on the subject. An incompetent person should never be allowed to judge or evaluate a competent one.

Listening to the youngster helps. If they know more than you, then gladly accept a role reversal—become their student. Teaching can be more fulfilling when it happens both ways. Teaching has always been an exciting learning opportunity for me.

When Curiosity Never Ages

My eighty-six-year-old father is a great fan of generative AI. He ideates with it and authors stories for magazines in Kannada. He is sharp as a razor to be able to use the latest technology available for his work. I tip my hat off to him.

He called me the other day and shared his experiences with generative AI and suggested that I do the same—use AI for my work. I didn't have the heart to tell him that it was useless to me.

The best synthesis of ideas comes from seminal ones. AI can help a little, yes, when one is looking for perspective. But original ideas triumph in the market; not ones that have been done to death on the Internet. Anyway, this is not an article on GPT-4. It is on my old man.

When Dad told me I needed to use AI, I didn't feel patronised. I was amazed by his childlike curiosity at that age. His thirst for new knowledge . . . his enthusiasm. I dared not tell him that GPT-4 has been around for many years, and I have explored it and found it to be ineffective.

Most of the content on GPT-4 is generic and always comes with disclaimers. We are not there, not yet. Happy to be a part of the journey, I foresee remarkable things for the future, and I am excited! I am not a cynic, and I believe that the world can be a better place as long as we keep asking new questions—like how to do something better.

Back to the topic. My parents are the ultimate intrepid intellectual explorers that I have known. My mother, when she was alive, would finish reading a whole Kannada novel of 250 pages in twenty-four hours—she would stay awake all night. She never asked my dad for anything other than books. She was a schoolteacher who inspired children; she was very much a career woman.

However, she always made time to read widely. No wonder that Dad and Mom made such a lovable couple. My mother never wrote a syllable. Dad, on the other hand, is a writer. He has successfully published articles and authored a book. At his age, making time to write and finding motivation is incredible! But he does it with relative ease. Because he was born inspired, like my mother.

I fancy a scenario where my mother is a literary critic, and my dad is the writer. What would have transpired? My mom would have said things matter-of-factly and dad would have retaliated with an eloquent mail beginning with 'Dear Madam'. He would have deliberated on why he was right, and she was wrong. The argument would never end. Why bother to go on anyway?

The Art of Selling: Convincing or Confusing?

When I was barely seventeen and in college, I took up a sales job for a short while because I wanted to make pocket money. My employer then told me, 'If you cannot convince a customer, confuse him.' This sales strategy might have worked in the eighties, but not today, when consumers are so aware and picky.

I have hated and avoided this selling tactic ever since. I don't sell wares; I am in the ideas business. Even then, I have always believed that being honest in any business is key to gaining trust and building brand loyalty. If I claim something, I better have it.

Confusing people when I cannot convince them is the same as shamelessly lying. It is duplicity and unethical. If I have not convinced a person in the first three minutes of the pitch, I am unlikely to do so later. Which is perfectly fine. You win some, you lose some. There are many more fish in the sea.

I might lucky if I am honest and precipitate a buy-in some other time. But confusing the customer using jargon leads to long-lasting bad blood. Why? Simply because people detest everything they do not understand.

People need reasons to do everything—even buying. Their needs may be personal or influenced. But at least one good reason is needed to spend good money. When I confuse the buyer because I cannot convince him, I end up losing the customer for life. Like they say, you can fool someone once but not all the time. Your competitors will get ahead thanks to your dishonesty.

In convincing my audience to like my book, I need to figure out why they will probably do so—what are their reasons for liking my book? What do today's readers like and prefer reading? I need to understand where they are coming from—what strata of society—and graciously admit my follies in penning this book when I get feedback. Without such rigour, this book is likely to do badly in the market.

By confusing them, I am being obscure, hiding the truth or disguising it with fanciful jargon that seems too complicated to understand but sounds very fashionable. Or I might want to write homilies to prove that I am morally superior and underplay the fact that I am less informed and less discerning than many of my readers.

Confusing people to get a buy-in might work well with people who are uneducated and less aware. But most people these days, even the less-educated masses in developing countries, are extremely aware—thanks to the internet. They will not loosen their purse strings when they suspect foul play.

Confusing people is easy. I just need to talk down condescendingly to people and make them believe that I am intellectually superior to them. On the other hand, convincing people is challenging. I need to have and offer something my audience wants. Taking the shortcut and confusing people will never grow an enterprise. It is counterproductive. But convincing people with genuine intent draws customers closer to me and wins their trust.

The Power of Suggestion

Elsewhere in this book, I have devoted a chapter to serendipity. I am fascinated by how an event occurs just when I am thinking of it. For instance, if I think of a friend and, at that very moment, I get a call from them. Many a time, I dismiss this as sheer coincidence. But it happens so many times that it is hard not to feel that there is some science behind it. I think what is behind this is suggestibility.

Being a 'thinking person', I often think of things out of the blue. These thoughts are random and have no great purpose. It is simply intellectual wandering. At that very moment, I switch on the TV, and I see and hear something related to the thought in my mind. There is nothing mystical about this. The eye sees 'what it wants to see', and the ear hears 'what it wants to hear'. My mind attaches its thoughts to what it seeks to know.

Richard Bach, in his book *Illusions*, describes that when you desperately want an answer to a troubling question, all you have to do is pick up a book—any book—and open a page—any page. You will find your answer there. This has very little scientific basis or empirical evidence. But I think this happens because the mind gets attracted by, and attaches itself to, occurrences that it is thinking of at that very moment. This is called suggestion, which can be very powerful and effective, especially when a person is highly suggestible. It gives the suggester immense power over such a suggestible person.

I am not sure if I have made myself crystal clear. So here is a scenario. It is one of the oldest card tricks in the world. Think of a card—any card. The magician pulls out that card from a pack of well-shuffled cards. That is because, before the trick, the magician would have surreptitiously suggested that card to your subconscious mind with his shenanigans and is pretty certain that you are going to pick that card.

This has happened many times in my life. I see everything, and I am fairly suggestible. Moreover, I tend to overthink everything. It is not surprising, then, that I am drawn to—or take notice of—small, inconsequential occurrences that relate to my thoughts at that moment.

This makes me feel that the event occurred as a result of my thoughts, and I am delighted. I even think that these events were conjured up for my sake, that I am special in some way. But that is just ludicrous. In psychology, it is called 'Ideas of reference'. Why would a news anchor on TV say the things that I, and not the other millions of viewers, want to hear? It is delusion, not fact.

Assuming that suggestions can be very powerful, it is better to stick to parlour tricks and use them to entertain and amuse people. But when this kind of power is used on gullible people, especially young people, apocalyptic events may occur. I remember how I was 'remote-controlled' by certain friends I made in my teens. Doing everything that they suggested—even minor felonies like vandalising private property. It was like I had no mind of my own. Such is the power of suggestion.

the [illegible] of it that very moment. These [illegible] suggestions [illegible] can be very powerful and effective, especially if a person is highly suggestible. It gives the suggester [illegible] [illegible] suggestible person.

[illegible] made [illegible] [illegible]. So [illegible] [illegible] one of the oldest card tricks in the world. [illegible] a card [illegible] card. The [illegible] pulls out that card from a pack [illegible]. That is [illegible] in trick [illegible] would [illegible] [illegible] [illegible] [illegible] [illegible] [illegible] the [illegible] [illegible] are [illegible].

This has happened many times in my life. I [illegible] everything and [illegible] suggestible. [illegible] I tend to overthink everything. It is not surprising then that I am [illegible] [illegible] [illegible] or [illegible] that relate to my [illegible] in that moment.

This makes me feel [illegible] as a result of my thoughts, and I am [illegible] [illegible] [illegible] [illegible] [illegible] [illegible] my [illegible] that I am [illegible] in some way but [illegible] [illegible] [illegible] [illegible] [illegible] [illegible] [illegible] [illegible] news [illegible] on TV say the things that [illegible] [illegible] [illegible] [illegible] [illegible] that [illegible].

[illegible] that suggestion can be very powerful. It is [illegible] [illegible] and [illegible] and [illegible] people. [illegible] [illegible] [illegible] [illegible] on [illegible] people [illegible] [illegible] [illegible] [illegible] [illegible] [illegible] [illegible] [illegible] [illegible] [illegible] [illegible] [illegible] [illegible] [illegible] [illegible] [illegible] [illegible] [illegible] of my [illegible] [illegible] of suggestion.

Section III

On Work

Certainty or Faith

No decision in life and work is made without making some basic assumptions. I am taking pains to write this book assuming that someone like you will read it someday. Otherwise, why should I go through the trouble?

In every decision I make, I assume that my goals are in earnest, my resources are enough, my time is available, and my skills are optimal for the task. Without these assumptions, there is no success. Assumptions are often the foundation for a job well done.

What is crucial for success is the accuracy of the assumptions I make. Let's say, you ask me to perform heart surgery. Assuming that I can do it is downright stupid. Assuming that I am a surgeon is incredulous.

I lack the skills and the courage to cut open someone's chest and fix the heart. You are simply barking up the wrong tree. On the other hand, if you assume that I can produce a well-meaning 500-word essay, your assumption is simply spot on.

This means that the set of assumptions that I make should clearly spell out the restrictions and limitations. What needs to be done is a careful process of evaluating the assumptions for veracity before even taking the first step. If my assumptions have holes in them, then I need to go back to the fundamental question—to do or not to do.

I actually learnt the fine art of making basic assumptions when I was working in a global consultancy company many years ago as part of the presales team. Among the first few slides of the presentation, I was required to delineate the assumptions that my solution was based on. I had to assume certain basic conditions for the solution to work—whether my software was compatible with the standard operating environment of the client company.

Similarly, when my journalism career ended and I decided to freelance, I had to make some assumptions on how to remain financially solvent. I had to assume that my family would take care of all my banal necessities like food, a place to live, and Wi-Fi till I earned enough to support myself.

I had to assume that in case of emergencies, I would have to dig into my savings. Fortunately for me, these assumptions turned out to be right. My family did and continues to be my safety net and my savings have been useful during medical emergencies.

Making assumptions is not the same as hoping. In fact, they are very different. When I wrote this book, I assumed that I would find readers because I know for a fact that I am a pretty decent writer who is original and articulate. Never did I 'hope' to find readers. My assumption is based on fact not belief.

Hope is belief and hopes are often belied. Assumptions are based on solid rock. They are based on reality and consider a set of statistical probabilities given a set of pre-existing conditions and known outcomes.

Assumptions and hope force us to evaluate our skills, resources, and the environment intricately before embarking on an endeavour. Assuming can be risky . . . but hoping against hope can be futile.

The Dual Foundations: Processes and Outcomes

Whatever you do in life, whether it's brushing your teeth or sending people to space, there are two basic ingredients that are indispensable to your work—process and desired outcome.

The process can be defined as the means, methods, techniques, metrics, training, resource allocation, planning, execution, value creation, and a host of other commonly followed steps actioned towards the desired outcomes that are produced in phases or as a whole.

I understood this universal fact when I read John Heider's *Tao of Leadership* as a student. The author explains the binary principle—yin and yang, the polarities that make the whole. A lot of the philosophy is about process and principle. In my words, they are process and outcome.

Unless you are dealing with occurrences in the quantum realm, a given set of processes always yields a pre-determined set of results. If I invest time and energy into a project, like writing this book and making it readable, then statistically speaking, I stand a good chance of getting it published. If I don't do so, the book will never get published. Simple, right?

But I ask myself what comes first: Process or goal? The common understanding is that you set your goals first and create and execute processes to achieve the goal(s). This is true in most scenarios, but there are exceptions. For instance, writing and me. I am a writer, so I write. I do what I am. I had no desire to publish a book when I started this essay writing project. I had time on my hands, and I wanted to express myself in words. Basic.

The idea of making it into a book and approaching a publisher came much later. I made a list of things that I wanted to write about and began with them. The process came first. Not the goal. When I started penning essays, I had no publishing goals. It was only after several essays that the idea that it could be turned into a collection that could be published happened to strike me.

But once the decision was made, and an outcome was quantified and planned, the goal helped me greatly with the process of writing this book. I broke it down into phases—weekly goals, monthly goals, and a deadline for manuscript submission. The goal helped me refine not just one aspect of the process, but all of it. The goal gave me purpose.

This does not mean that all things can be accomplished without first setting goals. It is the magnitude of the task that decides what comes first. My book is not something people cannot live without, but if you are defending your nation, then you need to plan the war and each battle laboriously—down to the minute detail, together with contingencies. Or else your soldiers' lives could be lost in vain.

Goal setting and process improvements need to go hand in hand. But the goal finally decides the process. If the goal is inconsequential, people who are leading the project can afford to 'disagree but consent'. Inexpensive mistakes and retractions can be tolerated. But if the prize is too big, too important, then the goal is supreme, and the process must be engineered and re-engineered to match the ultimate outcome.

The Philosophy of Crisis Survival

Life is largely unpredictable. Many events surprise us and catch us unawares. However, there are also several things that point to the outcome with certainty. Following good advice on how to pre-empt inappropriate circumstances is always better.

Better safe than sorry.

When I was working in a global IT firm many years ago, my boss, a vice-president, came up with a grand idea that he called the 'scenario building initiative'. My team and I were asked to generate a range of scenarios, from terrorist attacks and fire mishaps to network downtime and an outbreak of malaria.

We were tasked with drafting manuals on how to handle such crises, which could then be proliferated enterprise-wide. These measures were intended to maintain business continuity. Post-COVID, many companies have evolved such protocols.

This got me thinking: How do we manage situations in our personal lives when disasters strike? Do we buckle in and wait for it to pass? Stand up and face the threat? Or simply run for our lives? In my view, these three options are worth considering.

Ask yourself how long the disaster is likely to last. Is it temporary or permanent? If it is temporary, then the measures you take will also be just as ephemeral. It would be wise to dig in your heels and hang in there until the danger passes. This is not unlike the recent pandemic, which claimed thousands of lives, but humanity as a whole survived it globally.

But there are incidents that demand urgent intervention and simply go away. For instance, a road accident. In this case, if the injured do not receive immediate medical attention, they will succumb to their injuries. This is a life-and-death situation where one would be foolish to waste time imagining outcomes. After the injured are treated, the danger has passed, and the situation requires little further attention.

The third type of response is critical. Many would consider it escapism or unmanly, but it has tremendous benefits in seemingly impossible situations. I use this avoidance method often in life.

Let's say I am a recovering alcoholic or a compulsive gambler. Would I prefer to tempt fate by being at a party where everyone is drinking until they black out or losing all their money? Why would I?

I always have the prerogative of not going to such a party or walking away from one. By staying, I purposefully put myself in danger. In such a situation, there is no shame in walking away. My very life depends on it. This reminds me of something that Bruce Lee said to a reporter during an interview.

The reporter asked Bruce Lee, 'You are the greatest martial arts expert in the world. What would you do if a robber with a gun stops you and demands your money and ring?'

Bruce Lee answered, 'I would hand over all my money and the ring, of course. I am not foolish enough to risk my life for money!'

Defining Your Own Triumphs

Consider this: Mount Everest can be photographed or filmed from every possible angle with remarkable accuracy using drones. But why do hundreds of people climb the mountain each year and take pictures of themselves at its peak? They can generate morphed photographs on their home computers and share them on social media. The technology to do this in minutes is available today. Yet they undertake the perilous journey to the top, risking life and limb. Why?

This is because there is a sense of achievement in ascending the world's highest peak—a sense of fulfilment, joy, and excitement. People who climb Mount Everest want their names to be etched in history as achievers. They attain a measure of immortality. Especially the first to do so—Sir Edmund Hillary and Tenzing Norgay. Their achievement is a triumph for all of humankind.

They want to feel the rush that accompanies achieving the seemingly impossible by taking on the challenge head-on. Barely a few such achievements make life worth living, satisfying, and inspiring. It brings the achiever the merit of having been brave, adventurous, persistent, and successful. It is moments like summiting Mount Everest that make life worth living. Once you achieve what you set out to do, something you once thought impossible, your entire life finds purpose and meaning.

Not all human achievement comes from climbing Mount Everest. Most achievements are quite ordinary in comparison. The fact is that they are very personal. What you consider an achievement worth celebrating may simply be a daily task completed for many others.

A peculiar example is that of an alcoholic who is an AA member trying to stay sober one day at a time. For him, each day he spends without drinking is an achievement. For the multitudes who are not problem drinkers, this does not even matter as something they should mindfully do each day. It does not count as an accomplishment at all.

But the sober alcoholic feels like a winner for the day. He is proud of the fact that he has one more sober day to account for in his life of recovery. He is as happy as a mountaineer who has summited Mount Everest when he celebrates one year of sobriety. In AA, they give him a medal for it—the only place in the world where they award you for *not* drinking!

A more common example is that of a person who sets a daily exercise or weight-loss goal and achieves it consistently for six months. They are jubilant when they achieve their goal, just as joyful as the Everest summiteer. The achievement augments their self-image. It drives them to take on bigger challenges in life that have nothing to do with exercise and weight loss.

There is something in humans that makes them more adventurous than other species—a need to achieve what celebrates the human spirit. Millennia ago, if our nomadic, hunter-gatherer ancestors had not ventured out of their territories as the population increased and food became scarce, occupying new continents thousands of kilometres away, humanity would not have survived. Since then, we have never looked back. Hundreds of thousands of individual and collective achievements have ensured that Homo sapiens rule the Earth.

No matter who you are, or what you do, if the sense of achievement is missing from your life, life becomes dull, even unbearable at times. Self-doubt and self-loathing will set in eventually. When you are on your deathbed and look back at your life, there must be at least a few achievements to your credit. Otherwise, you go with regret.

Each of us has a frame of reference regarding personal achievement. Some people set very high expectations for themselves, while others are content with completing ordinary tasks consistently. What matters is not other people's lofty goals and accomplishments. It is your victories . . . after all, you are your own judge on judgement day.

Reimagining Moral Science

When I was in school in the 1980s, we had a subject that we would face an examination for, Moral Science. I know this sounds funny to Gen Z. What the heck is moral science anyway? What do they teach? The Bible, Quran, or Gita? What kind of questions do they ask in the exam? How does one prepare for this exam? Finally, does it even matter? What happens when one fails this exam?

For starters, moral science was introduced as a subject by the state education department to train students to make ethical choices in life. It was meant to help students distinguish between right and wrong. To grow up with Indian values like honesty, hard work, and prudence.

But the textbook for this was interesting. It contained stories from *Panchatantra*, *Aesop's Fables*, and a few anecdotes of the Ramayana and Mahabharata—two of the greatest epics of Hinduism. Now the subject does not exist in school syllabi. Even parables from the Bible like the 'Good Samaritan'.

I wonder if this really shaped my personality because I am clearly very different from what the morality-embedded stories were meant to make me. Although, I appreciate the idea of it. If you think of it, this was a great opportunity to mould character in young minds.

If I remember correctly, the moral science I learnt was not religious dogma. It was about value systems—Telling right from wrong and living a spiritually inspired life. It was about right thought and action. It was definitely all about karma and very understatedly stressed the fact that good karma results in good and bad karma results in bad—the way little kids understand.

I remember that the textbook had illustrations making it easy for the students to comprehend difficult values graphically. The textbook was about 100 pages in all with many sketches. And this subject, unlike math and science, was a graded one. Meaning there were no percentages in the answer paper evaluation—only A, B, C grades.

Since we have a value-inspired country now, I wonder why the government(s) have not tried to reintroduce moral science as a subject at the middle school level. It may not work as well at the high school level because today's 'Googling' kids will reject it outright as irrelevant. But by then, the foundation is laid.

If terrorist outfits can brainwash and train five-year-old children to fight jihad, why can't we, in India, openly, statedly, train our kids in our value systems in kindergarten and middle school? What harm can it do after all? We as a country have been pacifists for eons. None of our scriptures preach or propagate violence and bloodshed.

Teaching moral science in school has many merits; and the attendant exam, too. Care should be taken to be liberal and not make failure in the exam a stigma. It can remain a graded test as it has always been. A 'C' grade must not mean that the student fails the course. In fact, that should mean that the student needs more moral education than the rest.

With all the technology available, moral education can become a national movement to inculcate values in India. We don't need spiritual gurus to learn what our values are. We don't need spirituality courses and programs if we as kids are tutored and raised in a value-based family and school.

Realising Your Potential

I find that in order to self-actualise and lead a meaningful life, I need not do everything that all others do but realise my potential only. To do that, I first need to know what potential, unique skills and talents I possess. In my case, it is mostly writing. However, to become a writer, if not a great one, I need to develop certain skills in my trade and build a career that makes me a writer of some significance.

My innate potential remains dormant if I do not learn new skills and put my potential to work. I can spend my whole life without using providence-given talent if I do not realise what my potential is, and don't apply my mind in that direction. My talents and capabilities remain unused if I do not introspect, recognise my potential, and make an effort to hone my skills through repetitive practice.

I find that each of us is gifted with at least two kinds of capabilities—ones that we learn in life and the others that we are born with. While the first is common to most people, the other is unique to me.

All of us go through school and learn what society and family expect us to learn. Simultaneously, we learn skills—

creative, intellectual, and social—at work and leisure. But the inherent skills we possess get sharpened from day one of our lives in a manner that is quintessential. This kind of learning is providential.

Let me explain. You may be an engineer, but you could be a gifted painter, too. You have to take a course in engineering to become an engineer but to paint you just need to make time and be inspired to create a work of art. The second skill is something you are naturally good at. You could take an art course, too, but even without it you can be a reasonably good painter.

This brings us back to something that I have written about in this book elsewhere—you are not what you do. You do what you are. Painting is not just your passion; it is your very personality. It makes you who you are. Arty. Engineering is a skill, a career. Painting is a talent or a strength. Your artistic nature is your soul urge and your work as an engineer is your life path.

I feel sorry for people who get caught up in work and family commitments and never get the time or opportunity to indulge in hobbies and make an effort to find out what they are naturally good at. Their latent skills and inborn abilities never see the light of day. They live and pass away that way without sparing a thought or asking, '*What if . . . ? What if I could act, sing, draw, or dance?*'

I consider myself lucky to have a career that is based on my innate writing talent. That way, I really enjoy my work—I never get tired or bored. I write because I am a writer. I was born that way. I do what I am.

I Am What I Am

No gift comes without a setback. What the good lord giveth, He taketh away. The Latin phrase '*Nullum magnum ingenium sine mixtura deminatie fuit*' translates to 'There has been no great wisdom without an element of madness.' The Roman philosopher Lucius Annaeus Seneca the Younger made this remark.

I find it true in my own case. I am not a brilliant rocket scientist, Machiavellian politician, a skilled surgeon who saves lives, or an astute economist who revives a dying economy. I am not any of these things. I am just a poorly paid writer, and there are millions like me.

However, I feel inspired all the time! My sole predicament in life is what do I do with this feeling? It makes me restless and empty when I am out of ideas to write. Do you feel the same? Or have you felt the same way anytime in your life? If so, then this essay is for you.

If something has been bothering you for years—an unfulfilled desire to do something—and you have either not had the time or motivation to achieve that something, then you must get down to achieving it right away. Like I did by authoring this book.

People will call you crazy and even stupid to pursue something that does not fetch money. Ignore them and carry on. You will have the last laugh, I assure you, if your intentions are in earnest. Do it for yourself, not for others and care a damn for what their take on it is. Do it for those you love.

Please allow me to ramble on a bit here. I am diagnosed with Bipolar, and I have seen magnificent highs and crippling lows. My entire life is dedicated to being a functional BPAD (Bipolar Affective Disordered person). But I know I am a reasonably good storyteller—whether I am telling a brand story or my own. I make money out of the former and find satisfaction in doing the other.

Every gift that you receive has a rider attached to it—that you use it for good. If used wrongly, your karma will catch up with you sooner than later, and rest assured that you will pay for your misdemeanours in this life, not the next.

Both the Hindu and Buddhist law of karma is ubiquitously perfect. It does not promise you heaven nor scare you of hell. It is simply cause and effect. It is all about facing the consequences of the choices you make in this life. Whether you enjoy or suffer in this very life that you have now.

Coming back to gifts received. I have only one gift: A way with words, unfortunately not with people, else I would have chosen to pursue a career in sales and marketing rather than journalism. It would have earned me more money than I have ever made in my life. I chose journalism because I like to express myself in words, not sales pitches and PPTs.

Gallup Inc. emphasises strength-based leadership. It is essential to identify your strengths and weaknesses and focus on leading with your strengths. My signature strengths are analytical and strategic among others. And the test proves that I am a learner for life. I care to individualise and customise my content to different people differently. This is who I am and will always be at the core. Being who I am is not such a bad thing after all.

Thought and Action

Every thought begins as a germ of an idea in my mind. It grows and develops till my mind is consumed by the idea. It is a precursor to a feeling, which, in turn, leads to belief and conviction. Action follows conviction. Be that as it may, this whole process takes only a few seconds. That is the speed of thought.

This, perhaps, is the process that every thinking person adopts. So, it is natural to assume that to act differently, I must think differently. It is hard to control racing thoughts, especially if one is an obsessive thinker like me. Thinking too much can result in 'analysis paralysis'.

In any given situation, I think many, many thoughts—some positive and others negative. But unless I command the train of thoughts, it is tough to obtain crystal clarity and act rightly.

Feelings often cloud the thinking mind—fear, expectation, anger, resentment, and a host of others that follow the thought. It is not easy for an emotional person like me to control the upsurge of feelings that accompany the thought. But this must be done to choose the right course of action.

I find that my value system also plays a major role here. My worldview of right and wrong. Values determine what actions I take and what I abandon. Thoughts themselves are free from judgment. It is my value system that colours thought and determines when and where to act, what to do, how to do it, and who to do it to.

For me, the 'why' is the most important element here. It justifies action and in retrospect, determines if the action taken was appropriate or not. Like Albert Einstein once said: 'Perfection of means and confusion of ends seem to characterise our age.' If I get the 'why' right, then half the battle is won.

Right thinking may not always lead to the best course of action. Circumstances may change at times. But, at least, I can be certain and unregretful that the best possible action has been taken; given the situation. This lays the imperative on being conscious of the 'now' (having presence of mind) and not going by my hardened patterns of behaviour.

I notice that clarity in thinking occurs when I am alone. The retreat into solitude enhances my thinking process, and the kind of thoughts that occur when I am alone are pure and untainted by situations and people. In isolation, solutions to worrisome problems emerge quickly and with utmost clarity.

Yes, seeking others' opinions in troubling situations is a good practice. But this is all data gathering, due diligence, and deliberation. But for the final decision, one needs to meditate alone and decide. 'Thinking on one's feet' all the time may lead to a slew of bad decisions that result in messy situations.

Creative Visualisation and Fantasy

There are differences between creative visualisation (CV) and fantasy. However, there is only a thin line between the two kinds of mental activity. One can easily become the other if I am not careful.

Creative visualisation needs effort on my part. Fantasy is a kind of mental escape that does have some minor benefits in easing mental anguish, but is mostly spontaneous and can happen anywhere, anytime. CV is deliberate. Fantasy is a boundless flight of random ideas and imagery. CV spurs action. Fantasy merely entertains.

For visualising a challenge, I need to create mental images that align with the desired outcomes. I have to actively put my wandering mind to work and focus on visualising the outcome as perfectly as possible. I need to expend mental energy and imagination to build a storyline that ends in success. CV is then subsequently followed by action. It always has a purpose—it is never vagrant or thoughtless.

When I visualise creatively, I examine the emotions that spring from a given string of thoughts. I use those emotions to propel me forward. For instance, if I am creatively visualising this book becoming a bestseller, then in my CV, I have to imagine a succession of events leading to that happy outcome.

I need to tell myself a compelling story. When I do that, the words I speak and the actions I take in my visuals program my subconscious mind to activate my conscious awareness.

Fantasy, on the other hand, is goalless. It is just an unharnessed string of thoughts that come and create emotions—good or bad—and go. It is usually a subconscious, unfulfilled desire coming to the fore.

Using the above example of my bestselling book, my fantasy would be vague, undefined imagery of adulation for it coming from all quarters irrespective of the who, why, what, where, when, and how of it. Here there is no elaborate story to tell. In this daydream, I am just celebrating. I might even fancily imagine hosting a party for the success of my book without even going through the construction of the litany of events that led to the success.

CV needs rigour. Here, my story needs to be brilliantly colourful but plausible. It needs to be pragmatic at the least. When it comes to fantasy, the wilder the better. If I feel like having aliens drinking champagne with me at my party, I am free to fantasise about it. Who is to stop me? It is my daydream after all! But is there a point in all this? Perhaps not.

I have used my CV and changed some highly undesirable habits that had taken deep root in my psyche. CV has actually worked wonders for me in the long run, and being the dreamy type with a hyperactive imagination, I fantasise. However, I have mastered the fine art of differentiating between CV and fantasy.

What I do is, script and create grand, mega movies of my life in my conscious mind filled with what to do and how to do it. Sooner than later, I find that the colourful imagery I creatively visualised, actualises. Sometimes, I get more than I imagined, and sometimes less. But the CV certainly bears fruit. And usually good ones.

Hard Work, Smart Work

With all this debate on the seventy-hour work week, one wonders if 'working smart' is the only answer. My personal take is that hard work is irreplaceable. Working smart only makes the output greater and better. Smartness is in using technology and prized skill sets to make hard work really pay or even profitable.

Working smart is also a lot of work. It simply means that someone else worked hard to make your job easier. It requires the development of new skills and technologies that simplify hard work, increase productivity, and save time, cost, and resources. Smart work is not really a substitute for hard work. It complements hard work. This is just my personal view.

Why is hard work indispensable? Because even the fastest and most efficient computers are no match for the human brain. Mind you, you are using only 10 per cent of your brain capacity; dolphins use up to 20 per cent of theirs.

Besides, people are not using only their brains for work. They use their hearts, too. The best AI and machine learning software available today cannot be pre-trained to 'feel' human. At least, not yet. They can 'think' a bit like humans, yes, but not feel. Your computer does not say 'ouch' when asked to work seventy hours a week. It does your bidding.

Consider this scenario: A man without arms and legs swims. There are such people in the real world . . . you might have seen his videos. What makes him do this? Inspiration? Motivation? Thrill? Willpower? Hope? Need for acceptance? Now, ask yourself if your AI can do this without its hardware and software!

Usually, hard-working people feel responsible for the outcomes. They are driven by a host of other feelings like sense of duty, belonging, and achievement. It could also be gratitude, fulfilment, and above all, the need for appreciation. They don't sit around and wait for AI & ML labs to come up with a machine that does their job for them.

Not surprisingly, it is the same hard workers who are the early adopters of breakthroughs in technologies even when it involves more hard work in developing new skills and working longer hours.

Moreover, their support staff also work hard to ensure that the work conditions match the increased demand for services. The investors also work hard and invest more to ensure high returns in the long run. Ultimately everyone in the organisation and ecosystem ends up working harder. So much for smart machines!

Actually, there is no such thing as working smart at all. There is no 'hard' work either. There is only work. Work is the empty canvas with which the worker paints their colourful pictures. They define the work as hard, easy, smart, high-output, useless, good, bad, and so on. The question is what does your work mean to you?

It is written in the Bhagavad Gita that the individual has a right only to *Karma* (action/work), not the fruits of the action. I am no expert on the Gita, but I wonder at the kind of meditation that has gone into propounding such a universally true tenet on work five millennia ago.

I have worked hard in my career and spent a lot of time with others who do. One thing that we all agree on is that work is its own reward. Not just that, a blessing, too.

Channelling Your Work Energy

When all other conditions are favourable, the one factor that makes the difference between success and failure is the energy you give to your work. Working energetically does not mean just working hard, it means that you build rigour into your work—your thoroughness must show.

Most of the tasks that precede execution require arduous work, not the execution itself. It is the planning that needs to be thorough, considering the risks, eliminating some of them, and providing contingencies for others.

Most of the demanding work is done before the work actually begins. One must be thoroughly invested in the math before the task commences. One must seek different opinions and procure and allocate resources for each stage of the project.

It also means that you must anticipate and improvise when things do not go according to plan. The velocity of decision-making needs to be quick in such situations or else the project can simply slip away from your grasp and become just another bad experiment.

There are two kinds of decisions—fixed and flexible. Fixed decisions have a finality attached. They cannot be changed going forward. If you fail, you are likely to lose everything you invest—time, money, and resources. All gone forever! What's worse is you lose the trust of people.

Flexible decisions are the opposite. You can dive right in, monitor and change your decision when required. You stand to lose a lot less in this case. However, these decisions are low-impact decisions as compared to fixed decisions which are high-impact decisions.

I have noticed that fixed decisions require way too much rigour and energy to plan and execute. They have long-term consequences. When I decided to quit my lucrative job in corporate and dive back into journalism, I made an irreversible decision. At 52, no corporate is willing to employ me now. Instead of two options, I now have one: Journalism . . . the only one!

A flexible decision that I recently took was to freelance as a content specialist for various firms in India and overseas. This decision is reversible. I take up projects that I enjoy doing and say no when the work does not excite me.

I can afford to be whimsical now. I enjoy plenty of free time to pursue pet projects like this book. Needless to say, I can switch my freelance work on or off whenever I want. This kind of decision requires far less planning and thoroughness. As most clients are usually in a hurry to get the final deliverable, such work takes merely a few days of the week; hence less energy.

Once I have made a decision—fixed or flexible, I go all the way to ensure satisfaction among the people I serve. Whether the work hours are fixed or flexible, when it comes to work, I am punctilious and expend great energy in ensuring speed with quality. It is just this personal work ethic that makes me sought after. Not flowery language and sweet talk.

Motivation Matters: The Quest for Meaningful Work

Motivation to do something comes only when the result is certainly gainful. For me, to get off the starting line, I need to be at least half certain that the outcome of what I do will benefit me. I find that if the outcome of my actions is not favourable, I am not motivated enough to carry out the task.

I wonder if this is true of everyone. I find that it is largely true of people. If you are not convinced that your work will fetch considerable money, recognition, or whatever you desire, then why do it at all?

There are some people who enjoy work for its own sake. For them, it is the experience that matters, not the money or recognition; or both. I admire and envy such people. They are uncommon. They possess the motivation to carry out any task without any sort of assurance that they benefit from it.

Working for work's sake, for the experiences that come with the job, is an admirable quality. I find that many such people who enjoy work for its own sake are perfectionists, too. They want to get it right the first time, every time.

They are not usually materialistic. They don't worry about the incentives the job fetches for them. They are committed, too—

their level of commitment is usually above average. They deal with people in a respectful manner and even inspire others to get more involved in the task.

Result-orientation is a must for the accomplishment of any task whether at work or in our personal lives. This quality drives people towards great achievements. But focusing on the outcome too much, to be motivated only by the gains of the task, can make the experience of working less enjoyable. There is a likelihood that when things get tough, I might lose motivation. And being no longer motivated makes me want to quit midway. Why must I continue working if the results are not favourable or unattainable?

However, people who work for work's sake can lose sight of goals sometimes. They can go through the motions, without stopping to check if they are on course or straying. They can be oblivious to the fact that too much work is getting done but not in pursuit of the desired outcomes.

They are so caught up in soaking up experiences that they do not realise that efforts are being made in a direction that does not yield the planned milestones. Their motivation levels are so high that the task becomes a pleasure trip without a destination in mind.

To counter this kind of situation, one must enjoy the job, no doubt, but always keep goals in sight. I am a person who does this all the time. Whenever I get down to doing something, I decide whether I should take the first step, by considering two things: 'What's in it for me?'" and 'Will I enjoy doing this?'

If the answer is yes, I will benefit from the job, and yes, I will enjoy doing it, then I feel motivated enough to go on. Else, I refuse the job. Many a time, I take up a task just for the learning that I get out of it. However, only when there is a humanitarian purpose and service is the only motive.

But I don't believe in doing work for charity. There is always a monetary consideration or recognition involved, which is not such as bad attitude towards work after all. It is human to expect to be rewarded for work in some tangible manner. I find that my motivation is high when I make money and learn new skills while doing the job. This, I feel, is the right mix for high motivation.

The Key to Success

For you to be even reasonably successful in any endeavour, you must undeniably have at least these qualities—a way with words and a way with people. If you have both, then whatever measure of success you desire is yours. If you have one of these qualities and lack the other, then it is time to find a good partner for your journey who can compensate for your lack.

I have read books and watched videos on being successful, but it is hard to nail down the two important qualities that success requires. After some thought, I have narrowed it down to this pair of vital qualities, though there are many other considerations like skillsets, experience, and commitment. But if you don't have either of these qualities, your chance of succeeding is seriously in doubt.

Being articulate or having a way with words makes me a good communicator and we all know how crucial that is to success. If I am articulate, I get across the message clearly, directly, and precisely. Moreover, being personable makes people like me. This means that they are willing to listen to what I have to say. Articulation and personability are must-have skills for success.

I may be a great speaker or writer, but my message is lost in the din if people do not like me and are not willing to listen. I may be a very likeable person, but I will fail if I don't know how to articulate what I want to say.

When I see or read about successful people, I notice that effective communication and persona are their greatest assets. People like them and pay heed because their messages sound convincing. All other 'guaranteed success' techniques are derivatives of these two qualities.

Such men and women artfully craft their messages to appeal to the audience and their delivery is compelling. They understand their audiences because they are good with people. They intuitively know how a person will react to the message they convey. They know the right words to say and to whom they should be addressed.

They don't waste words or break relationships without reason. They know what their audience genuinely wants to hear and communicate with clarity and purpose. Their words seem inspiring to many.

Some people are popular but not taken seriously. This is not the category I am speaking about. Popularity can come instantly and for several wrong reasons. The people I refer to are successful, respectable, and true to their words.

They care for people whom they cross paths with. Above all, they do not lie. This means they are trustworthy all the time. Thankfully, the world has many such individuals who are great with words and people.

Having both—a way with people and a way with words—is an uncommon gift. This is why those who don't possess either of these sterling qualities need others to succeed. I have gladly partnered with many who are good with people. I assume I am good with words, and I have succeeded for both of our sakes.

Having a way with words and not with people makes me seek out partners who are, and I have been fairly successful and lucky in this regard.

Work Must Be 'Seen' to Be Done

I had a boss who once said, 'It is not enough if work is done. It must be seen to be done.' I have found this to be true in almost every work-related scenario. It simply means that you must deliver the goods within agreed timelines consistently till others take notice. It doesn't, however, mean that you should pretend to be busy all the time.

In any work environment, there are milestones and deadlines for each project. When you continuously achieve these milestones, over time, people will sit up and take cognisance of the fact that work is indeed getting done. The people close to you are the first to notice this. Then the bosses also get to know about it, and that is when the appreciation flows in.

Consistency is the key to getting work recognised. One must be at it whether one is lauded for the work. It is a bit of a waiting game. When you are relentless, you prove your sincerity and commitment. It is this sincerity that shines through, not the work per se. Even if you are falling short of the agreed list of deliverables for a while, people appreciate your perseverance in 'getting there'. I always lay a claim to progress. Not perfection.

Many times, your milestone achievements go unnoticed and unappreciated. Not because people are conspiring against you, but because your bosses are too busy with other things. Most senior executives in any organisation head many departments and can be too hassled to keep track of the work of just one team.

In such a case, it is a clever idea to intervene and make your achievements known. If you measure and document all that you do, this task becomes easier. You can share the progress reports with your supervisors via a few e-mails and ensure your work gets acknowledged. This is not blowing your own trumpet. It is a standard progress reporting practice.

The other thing you could do is get people who are close to you to start talking about the decent work done. If the workplace is abuzz with the talk of your achievements, then the word will certainly reach your bosses' ears soon. However, do this not just for yourself but for the team. It is a healthy practice to let people know that you have done splendid work because it boosts team morale.

Getting people to 'see' your work is essential for maintaining the momentum of execution. If excellent work goes unappreciated repeatedly, disappointment and apathy build up among team members. They may feel neglected and sidelined, and their spirits tend to dip.

A 'what difference does it make?' kind of feeling will immediately dampen their enthusiasm. I have experienced this in my career several times mainly because, wherever I went, I have always been at the bottom of the organisation's food chain. I never held any elevated position. I had little access to senior leaders and most of my work went unacknowledged.

But for the sake of the small teams I led, I made it a practice to generate periodical progress reports with analytics to back my claims and mailed them to senior managers in multiple departments—irrespective of whether they got back to me with appreciation or not. I made sure that even if no one is thankful for my team's performance, I would always have the evidence to show that work was done, measured, and reported widely across the enterprise.

The 99 Per Cent Syndrome

I have often observed that I am a victim of what I call the '99 percent condition'. It is commonly experienced when you are downloading a big file from the Internet or charging your mobile phone.

It takes less than thirty minutes to charge up to 99 per cent and then it seems that the last one percent charging takes forever. You are stuck at 99 per cent for the next half an hour. The same happens when you are downloading something substantial.

It takes only a few minutes to download the file up to 99 per cent, and then it takes so long to complete that you get frustrated. I will not go into the technological details of why this happens because I am not a techie. I am sure that all of you have experienced this.

However, when I think of it, many things in life are similar to this 99 per cent syndrome. Take this book, for instance. I needed less than two months to write eighty essays, and it has taken me one month to author the remaining ten. I noticed that the slowdown was not because of laziness or because I ran out of ideas to write on. The condition is essential to the process.

It is just like speeding on the highway and hitting a red light at a traffic junction. The completion of the task becomes excruciatingly slow. I reckon this happens for a reason.

When the mind is enthusiastic and charged, the momentum of the work will naturally quicken because everything about the experience (task) is new and exciting. There are so many things to gain—new learning, new people, and new challenges.

But when things become rote, and you do the same things more often, the mind succumbs to fatigue or boredom. This is an ordinary human predicament. Finally, as I approach completion of the task, I would have slowed down so much that it takes forever to complete it. Unless I jump the red light and get caught by the cops. The task loses its novelty without me noticing it.

What is the way out of the 99 per cent syndrome? Methinks it is simply grit that accomplishes the task. One needs to actually speed up and clear the red signal before it turns red. You need to accelerate not decelerate. That way, you will have more time to review your work and not default on the deadline.

Accelerating means putting more energy into my work. If I catch myself slacking, I need to garner the strength to carry on at the same pace as earlier, which requires extra effort and more hard work because there is no excitement or novelty anymore. Persistence is the only way forward.

The next time, the 99 per cent syndrome hits you, floor the gas pedal. Speed past the red light. Don't slow down. Clear the signal. Anticipate it happening. And you will not regret the extra work that you put in to finish the task. In hindsight, you will be proud of yourself because you kept your commitment to your customer. And you will have achieved it without getting caught for signal jumping.

The Procrastinator's Paradox

In a recent study conducted in a US university, over 70 per cent of the students admitted that they procrastinate and fear that it affects their careers adversely. Procrastination occurs when people assume they have ample time till the deadline and can rush it at the last moment. Like me. I am a terrible procrastinator.

Here is an illustration from my time as a university student. I have never really prepared for a graduating examination for a long time. Ever in my life, actually. All five of the gold medals I have were earned through intense cramming in the last week or two before the final exams.

While it is awesome how much work gets done in the last moment; procrastination has no solid justification. It is a setback anyway you look at it; especially, if it is a habit—a behavioural pattern that recurs.

The funny thing about procrastination is that most procrastinators already know what they should be doing rather than what they are doing now. They are fully aware that every lost minute is detrimental to them. And yet they procrastinate. Clever time-management skills bandied about on the internet are of little use when the procrastinator is busy looking for excuses.

People procrastinate when they are distracted from the task at hand. I am a champion at that. When I am hypomanic, I jump from one task to another with startling speed.

Procrastination also occurs because I am anxious about the outcome of the endeavour. When I become apathetic toward the cause, I think, 'There is only a 30 per cent chance that I will succeed. Why risk it?' Seriously? people with cancer who have a 10 per cent chance of cure, live on after treatment. What does one say to that?

Being risk-shy is one of the main reasons behind procrastination. It might not always be a personal foible, as there could be universal delays like when the pandemic struck.

So, how does one overcome procrastination?

The answer is simple to me because it worked in my case: 'Find purpose and means will follow,' as M. K. Gandhi said. Once you nail down your purpose on this planet—your very passion, mission, or profession—procrastination ceases to be a problem for you. Time—hours, weeks, days, and years will pass without you noticing it or complaining.

When I have my bearings, the path ahead becomes easy for me. I will commit to the task with conviction, and, when that is done, I know in my heart that I am a winner. It would be helpful to celebrate small wins while not losing sight of the ultimate destination. But when I love what I do, I will enjoy every bit of the journey. That is the secret that beats procrastination.

For the record. I thought of this topic for my book—procrastination—a day before writing it. I had planned to spend the entire day today watching dumb Hollywood movies on TV. But my urge to write this piece was so strong, I was so motivated, that I switched off the boob tube and got back to writing.

Why? Because I really wanted to write this essay. I had purpose, I had the time and the inclination. But the true reason is I knew that I would enjoy it.

Find your Ikigai and beat procrastination now!

Windows of Opportunity

My friends in a self-help group that I was part of a long time ago always said, 'Brother, when all doors for you are shut, remember God opens a window for you.' I really didn't understand what that meant until much later in life. I have benefitted from, and even monetised, many such 'windows of opportunity' since then.

When life is a roller-coaster ride for many of us, we despair. And in all that frenzy to hang on to a straw while drowning, we become scared, confused, and thoughtless. Most of our reactions are instinctive responses—fight, flight, or freeze. We seldom see a window of opportunity that could not only put us back on our feet but ensure that we become capable of handling such crises in the future with resilience.

We miss seeing those opportunities that seem highly risky, and unaffordable at first, and only come to fruition after the fight. We miss 'different'. The history of startups across the world, especially tech ones, has proved that 'different' can be good.

I don't want to waste words giving examples of the bold and the beautiful of the world—stories that have been told time and again and done to death.

I take my own example: I don't pontificate, I share. Generative AI not only revolutionised the content market, it wrecked lives, including mine. I had to fight a battle that was very personal to survive in the content creation market, and that was daunting.

I chose my strategy carefully. I remained *original.* When most content providers across the country were copy-pasting from websites, I made it my solemn duty to provide 100 per cent original content. I won in the end, but not without a fierce fight.

The first step was to monetise my connections. Most of what happened was by accident. And I got help when I needed it the most. Old friends put me on the launch pad and helped me get some assignments, many of which paid handsomely. This snowballed into relationships that fetch me repeat orders.

My experience is not unique. There are many who have walked down this path post-pandemic. There is always a glimmer of hope. The sun rises even when you don't. Nothing lasts, not even hardship. Life goes on even when you think it has ended for you. Be prepared to give life another chance.

Crafting Impactful Content

I am not a great writer. But I, as a news reporter and editor, have spent a lot of time writing and editing. So, I know what makes good copy and what does not—that much only. We live in the age of a social media revolution. Creating content is key to engaging audiences. In this world where strangers meet in cyberspace, your content makes you who you are. Whatever the size or form—text, images, videos, audio, and so on.

Creating content for impact begins with assessing and understanding what your target audience wants. I have written thousands of words in my twenty-eight-year career as a journalist. But people have read me only because they know me. The ones who really appreciate my content are mostly people who know me. This is no longer true.

However, I belong to the bygone era of print journalism. I confess that my content is not doing so well in the digital space. Because I have not bothered to gear up.

Hence the question—can we bring some best practices of the bygone print era to the digital world? I will not dare attempt to belittle social media evangelists and specialists. But one thing that is true of both traditional media and social media is the attention paid to detail. If your content lacks details and nuances, then it will fail to impress.

The second is brevity. I find that long posts on the internet, especially longer than 500 words, harness little attention. Blogs that are longer than that lose the reader midway through. And videos that are over three minutes in length fail to keep the viewer's attention.

It is another matter that a 1.5-hour movie in a theatre keeps the viewer glued to the screen. Like the first mass communication scientist Marshall McLuhan said: 'The medium is the message.' People come to a movie expecting it to be that long.

I have dabbled in social media content creation for many years now. Because I am forced to stay in step. I will never begin the shoot without a well-vetted script. Moreover, I always keep my target audience in mind when I write the script.

Social media have made people extremely powerful. You can now choose to watch a reel or not with the flick of a finger. And AI has made it convenient for you to choose what kind of videos you like by taking on the responsibility of choosing for you.

The third hack is making your content error-free, factually and grammatically. If your page does not appear true, you come across as someone with an agenda and your audience shrinks drastically. You are likely to cater to a notably lower population. You need to democratise your media.

I have noticed that in their bid to get more followers and likes, people often do shocking things in their posts. This will not last unless it is 'pleasantly shocking'. I have also noticed that using some measure of humour makes the video go viral. If being humorous is your goal, then you are in step. Posts in bad taste have an extremely short shelf-life. Today's audiences, even the young ones, are highly picky.

Finally, your content has to be unique. The message in it must be real and distinctive. This advice trumps everything else. If you post something because it is trendy, your message is lost and mired in the trend. I know that much.

Whatever the medium, your content is accepted at face value because audiences are hard-pressed for time. In such a scenario, maintaining simplicity in articulation is perhaps the most helpful advice I have received thus far. Keep it simple and you will be rewarded with appreciation for it.

Information, Knowledge, and Wisdom

People can steal my wealth, malign my reputation, and even take away my freedom, but the one priceless gift I possess—knowledge—is something that nobody can snatch from me. If you think deeply, the knowledge that is gained is for life. It remains even when all else that belongs to me is gone.

How is knowledge acquired? It begins with some data that I gather. When the data is inferred, it becomes information. When information is put to work, it becomes knowledge. When knowledge is shared, it turns into wisdom.

Being knowledgeable is being powerful; though in today's world, information is considered power. But having knowledge is superior to understanding. It is conflated and curated with human intuition and work experience. I could be well-formed, but that is not enough. I need to use the information in my daily work to create knowledge. From there on, it is mine for life.

Information and skills can be learnt by anyone who has a liking for the craft. However, I become knowledgeable only when I master those skills and digest all the information that I gather. And all mastery comes with practice.

This is why I speak of knowledge and expertise in the same breath. We tend to regard people as experts only when they possess the knowledge that comes with years of hard work using the skills they have. But to be wise, I must share my knowledge with others.

When I was a kid, most 'knowledgeable' people were usually old. This is not the case now. My elders were considered knowledgeable because they were well-read and highly qualified with many degrees to their credit.

Now, knowledge means 'exposure' to the internet. If you are on the internet (social media) bandwagon and trending, you are an expert or a knowledgeable person. You can teach master classes online, whatever your age.

This is by no means a bad development. I am thrilled by the ways in which information, knowledge, and wisdom are consumed online. I consider it the democratisation of knowledge and learning, which is a wonderful phenomenon. But I am also sad that books and newspapers have taken a backseat . . . perhaps I am old school.

However, I am distressed by the way false and useless information is shared online. Not just the ones that are factually incorrect, even those that reek of hate. All knowledge was originally gained and shared for noble causes. That was the only rider—that knowledge be used for the good of humankind.

'Knowledge for good' was the paragon of virtues among knowledgeable people not many years ago. Sadly, now, it pains me to witness the widespread vilification of knowledge. A lot of the 'knowledge' that is shared on social media is intended to mislead people. Additionally, because young people are the majority of the consumers of such information, it scares me. I feel that this will automatically lead to another revolution for the dawn of wisdom.

A Walk in the Park

Whenever I think of personal achievements, I am reminded that it was an outcome of pushing beyond my limits somehow. I realise that my success was the result of mustering courage and tenaciously pressing on despite failures and disappointments. I realise that what makes the difference between success and failure is attitude. I call it the 20 per cent stretch—achieving 20 per cent more than what I persistently can do presently.

A 'can-do' attitude is vital for success. But all success results from breaking through the mental barriers. It involves strength, resolve, and perseverance. There are no shortcuts to lasting success, though one can devise workarounds to achieve it sooner and better.

Let me illustrate with a small, personal example. I go for walks every morning and sometimes in the evening, too. I have a goal of brisk walking for 5.5 km a day. This takes me over an hour, and I burn approximately 320 kcal during the workout. I have been doing this every day for two months now.

However, I was unhappy that I was not able to raise the bar in terms of completing my daily goal in one hour. In order to improve my workout, I needed to walk all of the 5.5 km in one hour and not more. This meant that I had to increase my average pace during the workout to 5 km/hour from the existing 4.5km/hour. All this is simple math.

I monitored and documented my performance for two weeks. I used two phone apps for that and realised that the key was to push my median speed upwards by half a kilometre per hour. There was no other quick-fix, magic remedy. I persevered and achieved it in over two weeks by making incremental changes in my walking speed. That is Kaizen for you!

The first step was to visualise the achievement of the goal vividly. Next was to get excited with the idea. Then I needed to analytically figure out a way. Fourth, to put it into action without self-doubt. Fifth, monitor and make course corrections. Sixth, to be patient with myself as long as I was making progress. Finally, I congratulated myself for the achievement and kept at it.

This is all about goal setting and achievement in a nutshell for me. Agreed. There are far more portentous individual and collective goals to be achieved in science, technology, business, national security, and climate change. Achieving these 'world goals' requires far more meticulousness than what I have suggested.

My personal goal-setting and achieving framework appears too naïve and simplistic when such ominous and pressing issues need to be addressed. But this is a reflective book on personal effectiveness, not about saving the world.

So, dream and colour it abundantly. Build up enthusiasm and devise a plan based on math, not belief. Execute your plan with confidence and measure progress periodically. Be patient with yourself . . . you are only human. Reward yourself when you achieve it. Keep at it and the next time you succeed, you will find that it is far easier than the first time—a walk in the park!

Section IV

On Lessons

Ego as Nemesis

Some time ago, I was working for an IT corporation. They did not throw me out of the job; I quit—within three years. I had a point to prove despite my inability to cope with the pressures of the job. I wanted to quit to prove to people that I could survive without the handsome salary and dependence on it. I was wrong. I realise that now—when it is too late to go back. In hindsight, this was the best job I ever had. I was, for lack of a better expression, an egotistical fool.

The corporation I worked for was a benevolent one. The company had sheltered many under-achievers like me for years until they found their niche. I could have stayed, bided my time, and become useful. Some alternatives were even provided to me, but I did not take them seriously. I was in a hurry to quit and prove a point—that I could thrive without the job. I was wrong. My bad luck started the moment I quit this job. My ego was my nemesis.

It is simple to understand that one single employee, one person, cannot take on an IT giant that puts food on the tables of 2,00,000 families worldwide. If they think they don't require the organisation, it is their prerogative. But this global juggernaut is not in the least affected by the career choices that one single employee makes. The decision impacts only the employee and their family. The organisation remains intact.

My ego at that point in my life was so overwhelming that I failed to see the error of my ways. At that time, I felt I could sustain myself on my own. I fantasised that I would. All that happened because I was haughty.

If there was one single reason why I quit the job, it was not because it was difficult or stressful. It was because I was myopic in my vision of my future. I was very confident that I would land another job—which I did. But it was certainly nowhere near the kind of remuneration I had received in the IT job. My next salary was one-fifth of what I had earned in my IT role.

If my ego had not come in the way, if I had not suddenly developed a sense of entitlement, if I had not imagined that I could beat the vagaries of the job market, or if I had not believed that I was 'all-powerful', then maybe I would have continued to earn well, do well, and be content.

Instead, I put a spanner in the works and ended up being regretful and miserable. This has been my folly throughout my career. The sense of entitlement that comes with landing a new job—one of the dozen I have worked in—was the beginning of the end.

At 53, I am now wise. But to what avail? Nobody will give me a job now. Too much too late. If I had not quit my IT job in 2011, I would have grossed a sumptuous salary by now—growing up the ladder organically. Is my ego so important to me in all this? I wonder.

Reflecting on my journey, I've come to realise that ego, when unchecked, can indeed be one's greatest nemesis. It can cloud our judgement, distort our perception of reality, and lead us down paths of regret. In the end, it's not the recognition or validation from others that defines our true worth, but our ability to learn, adapt, and grow from our experiences.

Facing Mortality

I do not remember where or when this question was raised, but it goes something like this: 'If you had only one day to live, what things would you do differently?' What kind of a stupid question is that? I really wonder why people are so enamoured by such death-related questions.

Let us assume, for the sake of argument, that my death is certain tomorrow. I would live today exactly as I live each day. I would eat, sleep, write, edit, work out, read, listen to music, watch TV, and spend quality time with family and friends.

The things you must probably do differently are practical ones: Call your lawyer and make your will. You might also want to pay off any debts (luckily, I have had none for a very long time now) because you wouldn't want to leave behind someone feeling cheated. Additionally, you should apologise to the people you have hurt—which I now do often, both in word and deed.

I would live my last day exuberantly. The one thing I certainly would not do is try to make up for lost time or regret anything in my life. I would go happily. I have had a good life, all said and done, and I have been luckier than many others I know.

I have seen on the internet that people romanticise their bucket lists. They take this hypothetical question far too seriously and try to impress others with their replies. But here's the real question: You've had your entire life to do all these great things. Why wait until your last day to do them?

Was it because you didn't want to—which is absolutely fine? Or because you couldn't—which is not your fault? Why make fear of death your motivation?

Life is real, and death—the end of it—is, too. It is as real as the sun rising in the east or the flesh and bone I am made of. It is as real as my imperfections. If I am forewarned that I have limited time to live, then I am better off than most people because, usually, no one gets such an advantage.

Real people don't go around hypothesising about death. They live in the *now*. Real life is forever in the now, whether death is one day or one hour away. Real life is doing what you do each day: Live, work, and play.

If you have not 'self-actualised' yourself all these years, it is highly unlikely you will do it on your last day. Expecting a miraculous transformation when death is staring you in the face is silly. This is the stuff of movies.

When the moment arrives, I will be kind to myself and regret nothing. I will go in peace because I am at peace with myself *now*.

For Myself, Not the World

From time to time, I set personal goals for myself. Simple things like working out, saving money, or writing goals. But me being me, I slip up every single time. I begin with a bang and suddenly lose all motivation. I go out with a whimper. What generally follows is disillusionment.

I began telling myself that I am no good, a failure who lacks the willpower or strength of character that is common among perseverant people. This self-critique hurts my self-esteem, and I give up completely. This has happened to me all my life. But lately, I have discovered what could work for me in this regard—picking up where I left off.

I was indisposed recently with a minor health issue and was forced to skip my morning walks for a couple of days. But after two days of slack, the motivation was gone, and so I skipped the whole week. One morning, I feared that I would stop my morning walks altogether. However, a little voice in my head said: 'It's okay. Just pick up where you left off.' I am glad I did.

After over an hour of brisk walking, my head was swimming in endorphins, and I felt that I could achieve anything that day.

My self-respect was back where it belonged, and I simply felt good about myself. I am pretty sure that many people can relate to this feeling.

Often in life, we are forced to give up the things we enjoy. Work pressures, family issues, illness—the list of constraints is endless. But when things cool off a bit, we often fail to remember that we have let go of something that was really important to us before the problems began.

Even when we are conscious of this fact, we lack the energy and enthusiasm to pick up where we left off—we are filled with regret. But the point is that this is just a feeling, like all other feelings—high or low. The prerogative is still within me. Feeling diffident doesn't mean I have to act that way. A small self-pep talk can be the shot in the arm that puts me back on track—and joyfully so.

The time that is lost is lost forever, but must I not focus on the present? Why commit mental Harakiri and be gloomy as though all is lost? It is all in my head. I am the master of my feelings, not vice versa. I just need to find the pluck to pick up where I left off, and all will be well.

Come to think of it, who really cares whether I achieve my goals or not? My goals mean much to me, yes. But who else cares? Nobody!

So, this 'picking up' thing is something I do for my own sake—not for others. The question here is: Do I care enough for myself? Or not? If I do, then I have a lot of picking up to do.

From Nothing to Something to Everything

Everybody goes through three stages in life—personally, professionally, financially, or spiritually. We all begin with nothing, move on to having something, and, finally, reach a point where we feel we have everything we want.

I am not referring to those born into affluence. They are a minority, often having everything they could possibly desire from birth. I am talking about ordinary, hardworking, middle-class people.

In the first stage, life demands a struggle. It's a time to find a job, save money, and build lasting relationships. Take me, for example: When I reflect on my early years, I realise that apart from a decent education and a master's degree, I started my career with nothing. I had no money, no property, no vehicle—not even a two-wheeler—and no influential connections. But I persevered and built a life and career for myself.

This stage demanded a great deal from me, but I was grateful for it. Every challenge brought with it valuable life lessons—experiences that shaped my character. This is the stage where character is built and skills are honed. These experiences laid the foundation for the person I became and determined the trajectory of my career and life.

In the second stage, I had something of everything—a decent salary, well-honed skills, leadership roles, a car, a bike, enduring friendships, and recognition for my work. I also began to build the connections that mattered for my job.

However, what I value most from this phase are the relationships that endured. Family and friends who stood by me during tough times are still with me today. With maturity came bonds that were built to last. This was also the phase of my life that people still talk about with admiration—my days as an intrepid news reporter. These were my wonder years.

Now, having entered my fifties, I can safely say I have almost everything a middle-class person could wish for. There's no need to list everything again; suffice to say, I am grateful.

The one thing I value most is my good health. I do not suffer from chronic physical ailments that often trouble others my age. At over fifty, I feel as fit as I did at thirty-five.

These three stages of life—going from nothing to something to everything—are common to almost everyone. What makes the journey truly fulfilling, though, is gratitude. That's not to say I never complain; I do, about the things I lack. But these complaints are minor and far outweighed by the blessings that make my life comfortable and fulfilling today.

Recently, I lost a dear friend to a heart attack. He was fifty-two, and his sudden passing was a shock to all of us who had known him since our college days. His loss was a poignant reminder of life's fragility. In comparison, I am not only content with my lot, but deeply thankful to simply be alive.

Despite the inevitable ups and downs, nurturing relationships and maintaining good health stand out as true markers of a fulfilling life. By cherishing these blessings, we can navigate the journey with a heart full of appreciation and a spirit resilient against life's uncertainties.

Know Thyself to Win

Knowing oneself offers far more advantages than simply acing job interviews. It plays a pivotal role in determining the career path you choose, the roles you are naturally inclined to excel in, the compensation that will keep you motivated, and even the friends you make at work.

Self-awareness also influences major life decisions: who you marry, how you raise your children, how you treat those who depend on you, and how you interact with those you rely on. It shapes your preferences in books, music, and films. In essence, success, happiness, and contentment in life depend significantly on knowing yourself.

What is your self-awareness quotient?

Having the right skill sets and experience is essential, but these are the things anyone can learn. Attributes like self-awareness, however, are harder to define and develop, as they are accumulated over a lifetime. Self-awareness typically improves with age, meaningful experiences, struggles, and joyous moments.

Here is a rule of thumb I follow: The percentage of self-knowledge (out of 100 per cent) you have acquired is roughly equal to your age. For instance, if you're twenty-five years old, you've gained 25 per cent of all the self-awareness you're likely to acquire in your lifetime. At thirty-two, you've reached 32 per cent. While there's no scientific study to back this up, it aligns with my personal experiences.

The role of self-awareness in overcoming challenges

Knowing yourself reduces the trial-and-error burden of life's challenges. To prepare, I often make a list of 'me as a person'—what I enjoy, respect, desire, dislike, or avoid. This requires reflection. Those twenty minutes of introspection, jotting thoughts down on paper, have the power to transform my perspective and decisions.

Once I feel confident about my self-awareness in relation to the decision at hand, I dive in and face challenges head-on—not by their tail. Among the many winning strategies I've encountered over the years, this one has consistently worked for me.

At fifty-three, I can confidently say I know half of what there is to know about myself. Yet, I am still learning. This self-awareness has spared me from many potential setbacks and guided me on a path to moderate success.

A personal lesson in self-awareness

When I was in seventh grade, I wrote an essay that received much appreciation from teachers and peers. At that moment, I realised my aptitude lay in writing, journalism, and content creation. However, I ignored that inner voice and chose to pursue a science course instead.

That decision led to failure, and I eventually switched to journalism, earning two degrees in the field with flying colours.

From then on, there was no looking back. If I had listened to my intuition earlier, I could have saved the time and money spent on the science course. But none of that matters now.

What does matter is that you are reading this book—my book.

Living Life One Day at a Time

Taking it one day at a time is the best advice I have ever received in life. When life is lived one day at a time, it becomes simple and beautiful. Many problems resolve themselves, and life becomes joyful. The one-day-at-a-time philosophy ensures that those sixteen waking hours are spent meaningfully and productively, and the night is well-slept.

Living life one day at a time does not negate the need for long-term thinking and planning. One must ensure that one's own and one's family's futures are secure. The beauty of living life for the day is that it gives you the opportunity to enjoy the present without worrying about the future. Once all measures have been taken to guarantee a secure future, one should switch to living one day at a time.

A life thus lived is bereft of anxiety. I do not regret yesterday or worry about tomorrow. I am always in the present—the now. I simply need to make a checklist of the things to achieve in that one day I have at my disposal and trust providence to figure out the rest. I just need to be committed to my daily goals and leave yesterday's and tomorrow's issues to unfold in their own time.

I find that living life can sometimes be exhausting, and anxiety makes things worse. When I am living life only for the day, I do not burn out. I get enough rest, and I am neither mentally nor physically drained.

Some things may turn out as expected, and many problems may remain unresolved. However, this lovely way of living ensures that I have some energy left for the problems that can be faced tomorrow. Living one day at a time buys me time—a breather. It brings clarity in thinking and problem-solving. Living one day at a time clears the slate each morning for a brand-new day.

The one-day-at-a-time way of life does not help much with matters concerning retirement, old age, health, and other emergencies. Without exception, I will have to think and plan for contingencies. I will always need good health, insurance, savings, and the support of friends or family. I still need to envision a comfortable life for when my personal income becomes zero. I need a survival plan for when I have to manage without external help.

One day at a time is largely useful and works wonders for people who have been—knowingly or unknowingly—living most of their lives that way. Just to be clear, take me for instance. I have never planned for the future at any stage of my life. But I still make some money working from home and bond strongly with my family. Moreover, I have enough health insurance and some savings. This keeps me content and comfortable. Even the people who support me understand that I am a one-day-at-a-time person and accept me as such.

I must admit I have been incredibly lucky. Others may not be as lucky as I am. But then again, tomorrow is another day.

Miles to Go before I Sleep

You are not what you do. You do what you are.

As a young boy, I liked to write poetry, and people told me I was good at it. In high school, I was assigned a story titled *Autobiography of a Cockroach*. It was so comically and interestingly written that the teacher asked me to read it aloud to the whole class.

Since then, I have written hundreds of thousands of words of original content. For me, writing, which began as a hobby, became a vocation and a breadwinner. Over time, the realisation that a career in writing was best suited to me became apparent. When it was time for me to graduate, I chose the humanities—a course in journalism. I graduated with five gold medals, which strengthened my resolve to become a journalist. After working for twenty-five years in various media houses, I now know I made the right choice in pursuing journalism as a career. My choice has been vindicated.

Why am I writing all this? Because sometimes, before we get to choose our career paths, our calling in life chooses us. It is only at an advanced age that we realise why we were compelled by our nature to make the choices we made. It is a lot like being remote-controlled. This also explains why we swap lucrative jobs for an untrodden path. I am the only career journalist in my large family; the rest are doctors, engineers, lawyers, teachers, etc.

This is the same kind of calling that turns a chip engineer into a policeman (there is one such high-ranking police officer in Bengaluru) or a soldier into a writer (James Clavell comes to mind).

Recognising one's calling in life is vital to success and fulfilment. There are many things you may be good at, but there is always one thing that makes you truly happy. When you engage in this activity, you don't notice the passage of time. Your imagination is fired, and you are at peace. For me, it is writing.

When I am writing, both my mind and heart are in it. I am oblivious to my surroundings. I am happy.

Another thing is that I just cannot get enough of it! I am a tireless writer and can produce oodles of content without waiting for inspiration.

While pursuing a master's degree in journalism, I resolved to make my writing talent pay. What followed was a slew of jobs in media and content creation spanning over two decades. I did not end up making or saving too much money, but I was happy doing something I excelled at. In hindsight, there is a sense of fulfilment. I have realised my potential to the fullest and continue to do so. I have no regrets about the career choices I made in my youth.

Lucky are those who find their calling and get opportunities to pursue it early in life. I dare say I am fortunate in this one aspect. Above all, I had parents who were not critical of my career choice. Instead, they supported me throughout my journey. I owe a great debt of gratitude to my family.

Many warned me that a career in journalism would not be as well-paid as one in software—which was the go-to profession in my heyday. But I realised then that I would never have been as happy as I am now if I had followed the herd. It was the road not taken for me, and there are miles to go before I sleep.

All my life, I have marched to the beat of a different drummer. I have never known stasis. While I am still evolving as a writer in my fifties, I know contentment and am free of self-doubt. I write not because I want to, but because I need to.

Moments of Serendipity

Maybe it is just serendipity or coincidence, but in my life, I have experienced it a hundred times thus far. The Bible says: 'All things come together for good.' In South Indian Hindu belief, the same sentiment is echoed. Our parents console us by saying, 'Don't worry. Everything happens for good,' especially when we suffer disappointments as children. Perhaps they just want to make us stop fearing failure.

However, as an adult, I have noticed through personal experience that this statement—that all things come together for good—is often true. Especially, if you consciously check its veracity mentally and can spot patterns in the string of occurrences that lead to happy outcomes. These patterns could, more often than not, provide solutions to people in distress.

Let me cite the most recent example—what happened today. Just before sitting down to write this essay, a friend texted me, saying he was looking for a place to get an MRI done. I was reading the newspaper and saw an advert for a diagnostic lab chain offering sizable discounts on MRIs. I immediately sent a picture of the advert to my friend, who got the MRI done for half the cost he would have otherwise incurred.

I am not a spokesperson for the lab chain. I just want my friend to get well soon. But the time difference between me seeing the advert and my friend's text was less than five minutes. Such experiences are so common that we usually don't pay much attention to them. But they happen to me all the time, and I am grateful for them.

Here's another story. I was hired as a consultant by the state government for a period to investigate the functioning and efficacy of its rural training institutes and produce a 100-page report on them. My name for the job was suggested to the agency by a friend and former colleague. There is nothing new in that—people often suggest their job-seeking friends' names when there is a vacancy.

It so happened that when I went for the interview, the director of the department, a bureaucrat, turned out to be someone I knew well from years ago. He had been a mentor of sorts, giving me stories when I was a cub reporter for a leading newspaper. We had not met or spoken to each other for twenty years!

I was startled when I saw him sitting there as the panel chairman. Needless to say, I bagged the opportunity, completed the task, and got paid handsomely for it. One question that still boggles my mind is: Why him? Why not one of the thousands of other bureaucrats in government service?

I could keep relating stories like this till kingdom come, but I think I have made my point. Coincidences are very, very common. But some of these coincidences make us wonder why things happen as they do, especially when you or someone you care about deeply is in need.

Being the helpful kind, I am always struck by how all things come together for good, often with clinically precise timing. Not always, but particularly when people in trouble need help. I dare not analyse it too deeply because I fear that these wonderful experiences will stop, and I will no longer be able to help myself or others.

Money Matters

I marvel at people who handle their finances well. In thirty years of earning money the honest way, I have yet to understand the nuances of this fine art of handling money rightly. I have now come to accept that I can't handle money the way most people do, save when possible, and spend wisely.

Though for most of my life, I have not had big money, there were jobs that I worked in that paid handsomely. For a time, I was earning more than I needed. But the surplus was never put into savings like most people do.

I blew all the money I had, mostly on things that I didn't need. Even now when I have very little money to spend, I tend to splurge all of it. So, I see that there is only one way out of it—accept that I cannot handle my money and leave it to someone else I trust.

In my opinion, handling one's money is probably the most important skill to be learnt in life. Being prudent in spending is the only way. When I see people handling their money, sometimes I feel they are being stingy. But the truth is they understand its value and the wonderful things it fetches to make life comfortable and well-lived. They realise the value of 'each rupee' as one friend describes it.

I have one such friend who values his hard-earned money. He grumbled when his son asked him Rs 300 to buy a 'colour changing' t-shirt. But he blew Rs 7 lakh on a vacation with his wife in Vietnam and Cambodia to celebrate their twenty-fifth wedding anniversary. He settles for less in daily life so that he can spend his money more meaningfully. Sadly, I lack this remarkable quality. I just want to keep spending money without any reservations and restrictions.

For me, money is earned to be spent. That kind of attitude brings nothing but trouble. For my kind of person, there is never enough money to spend. If you are a middle-class person like I am, that is a lifelong predicament. Unless you learn how to save.

The only other alternative is allowing someone else you trust to handle your money and subsist on a daily or weekly allowance. That way you don't waste money. You will be forcibly disciplined to save for the things you really need.

Now that periodic allowances have become a habit, I can feel secure enough without cash in my wallet. It is true that lack of money can cause anxiety and emotional insecurity. By letting someone prudently handle your money, the heavy responsibility of saving is taken off my shoulders.

I can rest assured that my supply of money is stable and continuous. Though not forever. I will eventually run out of cash unless I earn more. But I will have money to spend for extended periods and emergencies. The success of this game plan is dependent on accepting the fact that I am hopeless at handling my money.

Finally, comes letting go of control over your money, which can be challenging initially. Your ego will always remind you that it is 'your' money, and you are the rightful owner of it. Humility is the key. A humble acceptance that 'I cannot handle money and letting go of the ownership of the money must not make me sad but grateful that I have someone much smarter doing it for me.'

Accepting that someone more prudent can manage our money fosters a sense of security and relieves us from the anxiety of mismanagement. This approach requires humility and trust but ultimately brings peace of mind, allowing us to focus on what truly matters in life. Remember, it's not about the money but how we choose to use it to enrich our lives meaningfully.

My Adventurous Nature

When I was in high school, I was an active member of an outdoor adventure club. I would go to different schools and colleges with my clubmates to demonstrate rock climbing techniques and garner membership for our club. I would perform shocking rock-climbing feats for a cheering audience like a trapeze artist at a circus. I have done this at least a dozen times.

Throwing all caution and fear of heights to the winds, I would perform a technique called 'inverted abseiling', which involves placing all trust in the teammate who anchors/belays me, letting go of the rappelling rope, and hanging upside down on a five-story school building. This is among the riskiest techniques in rock climbing, which has since been shunned because it is dangerous and prone to disaster caused by human error.

In the last four decades, I have often recalled these experiences. What makes a teenager risk life and limb for applause? I have done almost no rock climbing since high school. I have been on treks, but of course, everyone does that, even people in their eighties. But what made me gamble with my very life?

One small belaying mistake, and I would have come hurtling down five floors to a certain, instant death. Some guardian angel was watching over me in those wonder years. If one thinks of it a little intricately, was this daring or recklessness?

Though I have never attempted anything as foolish as inverted abseiling in adulthood, in hindsight I realise that high-risk pursuits that endanger my health, finances, relationships, and career have always been an integral part of everything I am and do.

I was a reckless person. Period. I can justify my actions by claiming that being hooked to the adrenaline rush has been a trait in me until recently—say, the last ten years. The truth is what I did shocked the daylights out of people who still consider me crazy.

In stark contrast, my life today is that of a pensioner. Home-bound with few friends and no workmates, flexible work hours, and plenty of time for reflection. In comparison to my rock-climbing teen years, my life today is pleasantly lacklustre.

Now my adventures are all intellectual. Exploring questions that boggled my mind as a teenager and finding answers to them with caution not to stray from the road mostly taken. With life zipping past me, I have no opportunity to risk my life like I did in my teens. What danger does a man who leads a reclusive life face other than the ones he creates for himself?

The gnawing fears that I need to surmount in my life today are all my creations. What brought them about was not my adventurous nature. It was my stupidity.

However, not all my present circumstances are bad. I am grateful for everything I have today. But I miss my inverted abseiling days fondly. When I do that, I don't feel old or dissipated. The very thought fires my imagination and makes me want to make the most of what I have.

Sade Sati: Time to Be Productive

Have you ever heard of or experienced a period of your life called 'Sade Sati' by Vedic astrologers? It is most likely that you have—knowingly or unknowingly. This is considered a bad time by most people who believe in astrology. But I say, I am enjoying every bit of it!

Simply put, this mysterious term spells 'life troubles' for most believers in Indian astrology. I'm currently going through Sade Sati as I write this article, and I've never been happier with my lot. I'm on a roll, writing a book of essays in 100 days. I feel overjoyed and inspired, and—most importantly—productive!

According to some websites, I'm in the peak period where things are supposed to get extremely challenging. Admittedly, I've had my share of troubles and delays, but nothing out of the ordinary. In fact, I've experienced setbacks and delays for as long as I can remember. So, what's new?

For those unfamiliar, what is Sade Sati?

'Sade Sati, also known as Shani Sade Sati, is a phase in Indian astrology that spans approximately seven and a half years. During this period, the planet Saturn (Shani) transits over three zodiac signs—the sign immediately before the native's Moon sign, the native's Moon sign itself, and the sign after it.

Sade Sati is associated with both challenges and achievements, significantly impacting an individual's life. Some believe it brings difficulties, while others view it as a transformative time that can lead to spiritual growth.'

The above two paragraphs are copy-pasted from random websites, so I urge you to interpret them cautiously. I'm not an astrologer or a believer in the so-called 'science' that purportedly uses mathematics to determine people's fate. It's neither statistically valid nor plausible when compared to real-life experiences.

But for what it's worth, my Sade Sathi has been incredible. During this supposedly 'troubling' period, I've achieved a great deal: I've written 192 blogs for a tech media aggregator and another forty-plus blogs for a marketing content company. I've penned essays for this book, newspaper columns, solutioned RFPs, generated and reviewed content for ten websites, edited a book, and ghost-authored another. Moreover, I've already been paid for all of it! So, where is the setback I'm supposed to fear because the planets say so?

It was my younger sister who first got me thinking about Sade Sati. When I mentioned to her that my Sade Sati period was beginning, she remarked nonchalantly that it would be the most productive time of my life. I didn't quite understand her at the time—but now I do. She had just completed her Sade Sati and was receiving the purported gifts Lord Shani bestows once you've survived Sade Sati and He leaves your sign.

It is said that Lord Shani is like a karmic school headmaster who disciplines you during Sade Sati, making you pay for your karmic shortcomings and teaching you humility and acceptance.

When He leaves your sign, He bestows wonderful gifts upon you—rewards you truly deserve after all the sacrifices you've made. My prayer to Lord Shani is that I am deserving of the gifts I'm about to receive for my hard work when the time comes.

Sufficient Substitute

You can never really get rid of a bad habit. As they say, if you remove the 'H,' *a bit* remains. If you remove the 'A', *bit* remains. Finally, when you remove the 'B', *it* remains. A habit—good or bad—can never be entirely eliminated. However, it can be replaced with another habit.

What exactly is a habit? Habits are patterns of human behaviour that recur at regular intervals. Having a habit means performing the same action at the same time daily, during moments when you are inclined to repeat those actions.

In *Born to Win*, behavioural scientists Muriel James and Dorothy Jongeward call such patterns of behaviour as 'rituals'. People employ rituals to structure their time. There are two kinds of rituals: Empowering and disempowering.

Empowering rituals are those that people call good habits, and disempowering rituals are what are usually referred to as unhealthy habits. This is common knowledge. I will not bore you by listing good and unhealthy habits.

What does one do to overcome or be rid of a bad habit? I have been struggling for most of my life to get rid of my unhealthy habits like smoking. All the things I have read online or elsewhere state that I need to practise several things other than smoking, like drinking water and getting daily exercise. I do both with unfailing regularity.

However, these hacks to quit smoking have been of little value to me because I have had the habit for decades. These strategies are ineffective in my case. There are indeed people who have greatly benefited from them and been able to kick the habit.

I wonder if there is another way besides the popularly prescribed list of things to do to quit smoking. I realise I can never tackle the bad habit head-on with willpower alone. I need a 'sufficient substitute', a replacement. It is evident from this that a bad habit can never be removed, but it can be replaced with a good one.

Humans, like most other animals, are creatures of habit. They crave rituals to structure their time. In the absence of a good ritual, the human mind will automatically fill that available time with a bad one.

For instance, when a person with a reading habit has finished all the books they have, they might turn on the TV to fill the free time available to them. In cases where substances like nicotine and alcohol are used to fill that time, the condition becomes pathological and results in addiction.

I have devised a method where I can cut down on my daily consumption of nicotine by using postponement. When I get the urge or craving, I tell myself that I will wait another fifteen minutes before lighting my next cigarette.

Sometimes, I tell myself I will smoke after finishing the task at hand. That way, I substitute my smoking with work. By staying occupied productively, I cut down on a few cigarettes I would have normally smoked that day. I have also had some success substituting nicotine intake with calling and speaking to a friend or taking a stroll.

I am not sure if I will ever be completely rid of my smoking habit, or when. But I am sure that someday I will find a substitute that gives me a bigger kick and satisfaction. I have known friends who quit smoking for life when they became fathers or mothers. Their love for their children was sufficient for them.

The Currency of Time

When I think of a commodity in the severest short supply, I find that time is the only real one. Money can directly or indirectly buy all other comforts and novelties. Time, and not money, is what I should desire to have sufficiently. Time should be the only real currency, I reckon.

Money can be earned indefinitely, and according to the Law of Diminishing Returns, any other commodity you purchase with money can only yield so much pleasure. The pleasure you derive from it keeps diminishing with increased usage. Time is the only commodity that does not lose its value, no matter how much you consume. I find that people who say 'buy me time' mean it temporarily or for an interim, not forever—because they realise, in reality, that buying time is impossible.

As we all know, everything comes with an expiry date. Not even the universe is exempt from this 'universal' law. Time becomes more valuable as you race towards that portentous date. Ironically, most of us have been given plenty of time by providence—even the terminally ill or high-risk category people. When they find that they have little time to live, they live exuberantly. I know I would, though I belong to neither category—thankfully, not yet.

After many years in journalism, I find myself living a semi-retired life with very few commitments and a lot of free time. Hence this book. My years in the media were hectic. I worked on weekends and public holidays, year after year, for twenty-five years.

I had little time to spend on myself, my family, reading, watching movies, learning a new skill, acquiring esoteric knowledge, travelling, and, of course, writing—what I wanted, not what my newspaper required. I didn't even have a routine that included a morning walk of 5.5 km per day (something I enjoy now). Thankfully, I now have enough time for all these things, and I feel blessed.

There are days I spend very, very quietly—in reflection and nothing else. I shut out the outside world, turn off the TV, mobile phone, and laptop, and spend hours thinking about existential questions, many of which I have addressed here in this book.

I may be totally wrong about quite a few things I present here. But one thing I am sure of is that I am grateful for the free time I have now. Free time is a boon, especially if one uses it for soul-searching. I understand that it is not a very fashionable idea compared to travelling the world on expensive vacations, but for me, the value of free time lies in the opportunity it gives me to understand myself and the world around me.

I would encourage readers to set aside a small amount of time each day for reflection and record their experiences in a journal. It may not mean much to you now, but when you reach where I am in life, these memoirs will serve you well. In hindsight, many things you thought you knew about yourself will seem invalid, and you will certainly discover new facets of your personality that you never thought existed.

Many years ago, during a job interview, I was asked by the panel what the job would mean to me if it were given to me. I said the most preposterous thing possible: 'It would help me on my journey of self-discovery.'

Well, that was the most inappropriate thing for a twenty-four-year-old to say in a job interview. But I got the job, didn't I?

The Power of Perseverance

For most of my life, I have been guilty of not finishing what I started. Now in my latter years, I realise what an idiot I have been. For the last four years into semi-retirement, I have recognised that this one lacuna in me has robbed me of a greater sense of being.

I now finish whatever I begin. You could call me a late bloomer. I started small . . . taking baby steps. Trivial things like achieving my daily walk goal, which is 5.5 km/day and a monthly goal of 100 km a month. Then bigger goals like sitting down with self-discipline and authoring an essay a day for this book—100 days, 100 essays.

Let me give you a glimpse of my life so far. I have worked fourteen jobs in twenty-five years—never sticking on when things got rough and jumping wherever I found an exit. A rolling stone gathers no moss, but a leapfrogging professional is sure to find himself unfit for employment when he is in his fifties. One must stick and make it work for at least three to five years to be deemed suitable for employment. This simple arithmetic was lost on me.

It takes pluck to stick and make it work, to finish what you have started. It is a marvellous quality, but it is common. Most so-called ordinary people have this capacity. In most cases, they are doing it not for themselves but for their families. They do it out of an ambiguous feeling called love. Can you imagine that?

It is this quality that pays the rent, children's school fees, medical bills, etc. Millions of people are not happy with their place in life. Lucky is the man who is happy with his place in life! But they carry on with only their commitments in sight like horses with blinds. I tip my hat to such people—the middle class, a category in which I was born and raised.

My unemployment dilemma made me think of alternatives—like writing this book. The real motive was relevance. I wanted to be relevant. To remain creatively occupied and be known as an author. There were hundreds of greater writers before me and there shall be hundreds after me. But what matters to me is that I was relevant for a time. All this is the product of being focused on finishing what I started—this book.

The way is to hang on to an engaging idea and make it work without wasting time. Time is the only commodity in short supply, everything else money can buy. Whatever the ambition, make a start, stick, and make it work. I wish there were an easier, softer way, but, unfortunately, there is not.

The Road Less Planned

There is a reason why I waited until I had completed writing thirty of these essays before penning the foreword for this book. I didn't know what to share with you in it. I find that in many life situations, we need to pack our backpacks and set out on the journey before we find the purpose for the endeavour. In this case, I began writing the articles before I had a concrete idea about what this book was about—existential questions.

I don't mean to belittle the importance of vision and planning, especially in high-impact areas like running businesses or countries. In such macro projects, each smaller project requires meticulous planning and flawless execution for it to succeed. Much more than achieving a monthly walk goal of 100 km (a personal goal) is at stake in such mega projects. Our very lives depend on the success of such ventures.

I know I would have fared better in my career if I had known for sure what I wanted, set realistic goals, and done pragmatic planning. But the importance of planning was lost on me back then. I still tend to dive headlong into the water before learning how to swim—metaphorically speaking. For me, there is no other way, because I realise that I cannot learn to swim by staying out of the water. And I am a fairly good swimmer, thank you.

But many times, in my life, I have journeyed without setting goals or visualising a roadmap for my pet projects. This book, a product of my intellectual wanderlust, is no exception. I waited for thirty essays to take shape before figuring out where I was heading with this book, and only then did I write the foreword. I believe that the endnote will materialise only after finishing the book.

People like me are common. Even people in high places, like intrepid entrepreneurs. They launch their startups having considered, measured, and forecasted very few variables of the business. All it takes is a good, doable idea and a whole lot of courage. The idea needs to be examined for viability, sustainability, and scale. In the beginning, all you need to know are the business and revenue models and risks. Then you are good to go. The rest follows.

As Mahatma Gandhi said: 'Find purpose, and means will follow.' Of course, there will be many false starts, iterations, and course corrections. But that is what makes the journey interesting and worthwhile. If you keep measuring your performance regularly and fixing bugs, you stand a good chance of success.

Personally, whenever I decide to do something good, I start immediately. Many a time, making a beginning is simply about falling in love with the idea . . . letting the idea consume my mind. Then the path ahead reveals itself. The more I work in the chosen direction, the easier the work becomes. By the time half the work is done, my momentum is so great that I often finish the project ahead of time.

Spending too much time analysing pros and cons and cost-benefit can be a waste of time. You do not have all the information you need at the beginning, and situations and market conditions are changing constantly. It is good to be able to anticipate risks. But I don't want to fall into 'analysis paralysis', which stops me from making a start.

The Sixth Sense

I find that people often use the words 'intuition' and 'premonition' interchangeably. However, the meanings of these two words are quite different—so, too, is the feeling they evoke. Intuition is the ability to understand something instinctively, without the need for conscious reasoning, whereas premonition is simply a strong feeling that something is about to happen. This is as simple an understanding as it gets.

An intuitive person relies on their life and work experiences to guide them. Intuition is deeply rooted in human experience. In contrast, premonition is an unscientifically explained feeling that something—good or bad—is about to occur. It is often characterised by fear or expectation. Being endowed with clairvoyant capabilities belongs to the realm of psychics, not physicists.

People who claim they can predict the future need to be transparent about how they go about doing it—but they seldom are. This field is rife with charlatans. Intuitive people, on the other hand, are common. Fortune tellers adopt a garb of mystery that awes their followers.

All my recent reading on intuition proves that it is a clearly present, working faculty of the human mind. Intuition is very much a part of everyday life; precognition, on the other hand, is a 'gift' that people 'claim to have' without providing proof. It is esoteric knowledge. The difference between an intuitive person and a precognitive one is the same as the difference between being highly perceptive and being a soothsayer.

Being a fairly intuitive person, I find that intuition is extremely useful in my life and work and guides my decision-making. It is instinctive knowing supported by the five senses. Premonition, however, is an unexplained 'sixth sense'—extrasensory perception.

Precognition involves predicting the future, often inaccurately or vaguely, as modern-day Nostradamuses do. I find that their predictions can be quite silly and are mostly false. In many cases, their predictions about themselves fail the test of reality.

I ask myself, given a choice, what would I rely on—my intuition, which has developed through my life experiences, is very much a part of me, and offers evidence of having encountered similar situations before? Or an astrologer, tarot card reader, palmist, or numerologist's predictions?

The question is: How well does this 'psychic' know me? I would rather ask my family and friends for advice—they do it for free!

To test whether a strong good or bad feeling is accurate, it helps to reflect and analyse past situations similar to the one you're in now. Only time can tell. When you relate present circumstances to similar past ones, what helped you more often—intuition or premonition? Did you succeed or merely engage in wishful thinking then?

Premonition is always a flighty feeling. It passes when circumstances change. My intuition, however, is a well of resources that is always with me . . . all the time.

The Weight of Resentment

I catch myself feeling resentful and vitriolic towards certain individuals who have hurt me in some way. I don't subscribe to the view that I must turn the other cheek. That is bullcrap. I need to get my revenge if my indignation is righteous . . . if I have been wronged for no fault of mine. If one is not assertive when facing a diatribe, one is a weakling.

I am not a vengeful person. Mostly, I let bygones be bygones and go on with life. But to take revenge, I must wait. Not wait and plot; just wait. Wait till I savour success in the things I work for. Like hip-hop star Kayne West famously said: 'Success is the best revenge.'

A bit of a flashback here . . .

When I was a kid, my father presented me with an illustrated comic book of Alexandre Dumas' *Count of Monte Cristo* where the protagonist, who is unlawfully imprisoned, chances upon a vast, hidden treasure and comes back as a count to seek revenge against the ones who imprisoned him. I am enamoured by this novel even now at this age. I simply love the narrative.

Success is the best revenge because it can do for me what I cannot do myself. As a peace-loving person, I don't have a predilection for violence of any kind—physical or mental. I value my equanimity and my ability to maintain centre and ground in all kinds of adversity. Resentment and vitriol damage my very soul.

I am at a point in my life where I must embrace all new and old experiences, people, comforts, blessings, talent, and recognition. I should be living energetically and cheerfully as I am running out of time at the speed of light. I don't have the luxury of being resentful, angry, and vitriolic. I need to consolidate my wins and introspect on my setbacks.

Whatever I do must impact somebody in a positive manner. I don't have to turn the other cheek and be pretentiously forgiving. I simply need to ignore people who like hurting me and my family and keep doing good karma proactively. Resounding success might seem elusive at any stage of my life henceforth. However, I must keep at it and remain useful.

Being angry, resentful, and vitriolic hurts me more than it hurts the other person. It is tiring and overwhelming. But mostly a waste of time. Why? Consider the rewards that resentment and vitriol fetch—the perverted satisfaction of giving it back—which is a highly temporary feeling. It passes just as fast as it comes.

Instead, when I do someone a good deed for the day, that person is likely to remember me for the good turn for a very long time. I earn their respect and appreciation for life.

What would you prefer?

Ignore the people who hurt you. You don't have to forgive them. You don't have to put up with them. Let them know you cannot be deterred. But mostly ignoring them makes them shut up!

Time Travel, My Style

Can one go back and forth in time? If you are a theoretical physicist, you will say yes. But if you are as ordinary as I am, you will say no. For the multitudes, time is linear and going back and forth is not possible. The past is gone forever, and the exact future remains unknown, except for a couple of statistical probabilities.

But I have discovered a 'new' way of time travel—in the privacy of my own mind, though I have no clue how to make it a reality. It is in my imagination—simply put, in my fantasies. People are even making money from it, calling it 'coaching in creative visualisation'.

In my fantasies, I can go back and forth in time. I can be my childhood superhero, marry the worthiest woman, be rich as hell, and do whatever I choose. I can create and interact with characters I have never known. But there is a very thin line between fantasy and psychosis. Psychosis is, very plainly put, described as a 'break in ties with reality'.

I have been psychotic many times in the past. But for the last five years, I have been episode-free. Still, I have the habit of daydreaming—vicariously living out those experiences I most desire in my imagination, rather than in reality. Daydreaming is stupendously easy. All you need is a hyperactive imagination. No money, status, skills, experience, or any of the usual qualities people rely on to become successful.

I have been institutionalised more times than I care to remember. But my hyperactive imagination just won't go away. It makes me who I am: Imaginative. Just like runners for life, I am a nutcase for life.

Let me take a moment to explain what actually happens in my head every day of my life. When I take breaks from my chosen line of work—content creation—I daydream. I seldom remember my night dreams when I wake up, but my daydreams are always with me. I can recall the entire storyline I construct in my head, even years later.

I dream of being rich, popular, and distinguished—the list is endless. None of these things happen, but I love the experience because it makes me vicariously happy for a few hours each day. In fact, I have come to *allot* a specific time of day for these reveries! I enjoy them as much as I enjoy my favourite meal.

Do I take these reveries seriously? Well, no. I'm not that mentally 'gone' yet. I try extremely hard to maintain my sanity and stay in touch with the real world. But these musings are my escape from the harsh reality I face now—irrelevance and the inevitable fading into oblivion, being totally forgotten.

Back to the original question—can one time travel in one's imagination? Certainly! I am living proof of it! I go back and forth, sideways, up, down, or at any angle I please when fantasising. It is *my* fantasy, after all. I can do as I wish.

I can imagine incidents sequentially in a linear fashion and jump back to the first imagined experience anytime or any way I like. I can then skip to the conclusion and revert to the middle of the imagined experience, dreaming up an entirely new sequence of events to replace the ones I don't like.

When I was young, there were very few self-help books to read. So, we grew up trusting one-liners—things people said about being successful in life in a single sentence. One I still remember is: 'People who dream the most, do the most.' I doubt the veracity of this statement. Dreamers keep dreaming, and doers keep doing. But I like the ring of it.

What is your take? I wonder.

Veils of Detachment

In the Bhagavad Gita, Lord Krishna says:

> '*Karmanyevaadhikaraste maa phaleshu kadaachana* I
> *Maa karmaphalaheturbhoor maa te sango' stvakarmani* II
>
> —Chapter 2, Verse 47

This translates to: 'Your right is to perform your work, but never to the results. Never be motivated by the results of your actions.'

I admit that I am no expert on the Gita, but this much I have realised:

The lord stresses that, as a man, I have only the right to action, not the outcome. Not to the success or failure. This is what scholars describe in oodles of prose as 'detachment'. Being detached is easy when you do not want something.

Say, I am a surgeon who knows nothing of the law. When I am in legal trouble, I go to a lawyer. Law was never on my career radar, and I seek expert counsel. But just suppose that I lose a patient—they die on the operating table. How does that feel?

What if, I am a teacher who is mentoring ten students and only one of them manages to pass the exam. I am a policeman, and I have not cracked the most sensational high-profile murder in years. I am a struggling artist who has never sold a single artwork. How am I supposed to cope with failure? With religious dogma? Renunciative philosophy? Must I then be ambitionless?

When a task I carry out ends in favourable outcomes, I have no problems with that. But when I fail, the blame game begins. I find multiple reasons to justify my actions and blame people, circumstances, etc. This tenet from the Bhagavad Gita reminds me that I was never in control of the results of my actions—good or bad. The lord decides that.

For a moment, I feel a discordant note here. If the same scriptures say that good action (karma) results in good results (*phala)* and bad results are the outcome of bad karma, then why do I suffer bad results when I have done good work? Moreover, why do so many people who do bad things enjoy riches, fame, power, and much more?

This is the pivot where I understand that I must stop rationalising. The lord divine has uttered that the fruits of action are His responsibility and will be bestowed as He wishes. Then why bother at all? Absolute lack of control means *letting go*—it means acceptance. To use a fancier word, it means detachment (from the fruits of my labour).

It is crucial to note here that the Gita stresses detachment and *not* inactivity. It does not, at any level, preach sloth. It does not rationalise my lethargy. It simply asks me to focus on work and nothing else.

Only karma—or action or work—helps maintain good health, wealth, and relationships. Everybody knows that much. No one will pay you good money for indolence. The Gita inspires individuals to work like no other scripture. It only asks that you remain detached while performing your duty and afterwards.

It takes upon itself the heavy burden of expectations. Expectations reduce the joy of life—especially when one fails repeatedly. By commanding me *not* to attach myself to the fruits of action, the Gita brings down my expectation meter from 100 to zero. It lightens my mental load like no other scripture. Do try it sometime. Let go of your expectations and complete your work for its own sake, and do it well. Do what I am doing with this book.

Change Is the Only Constant

Change is inevitable. Change is the only constant. I have heard people say this all the time. But have I changed over time? I wonder. I am the kind of person who adapts quite well to changing circumstances, even with things that are hard to cope with.

All said and done, I feel I have changed and evolved into a better person than I was ten years ago. The question is: Why did I change? Because my very life depended on it. There was no option to resist the changes that occurred in my life over the past decade.

There are very few things about me that have remained the same. I no longer have a salaried job, so I had to make lifestyle decisions to save money and reduce spending. My daily routine has changed to remain occupied constructively during all the free time I now have.

My relationships have improved as I became less aggressive and more considerate and loving. My circle of friends changed—actually, it widened—when I launched my own freelance writing venture. Even the way I dress has changed because I don't go out to work anymore. I work at home.

Moreover, world events also force people to change—like the pandemic and the advent of generative AI. Both these developments cost me dearly. I lost a lot of business because of these occurrences. I am now forced to settle for lesser compensation for assignments that I take up.

I find that, in my life, resisting change has been futile. Changes occur whether I like them or not. I have two choices—resist or adapt. By resisting, I waste time, energy, and money, causing myself unnecessary misery. What am I trying to prove? That I am invincible?

However, by adapting, I ensure that the hardship caused by the changing circumstances can be made bearable, even enjoyable. Adapting to change brings with it many gifts—such as new learning. I need to be more open-minded and willing to learn new skills, gain new knowledge, and approach experts for more insights. This is the thing about change that I immensely enjoy—getting new opportunities to learn more.

Soaking up new experiences during change has always fascinated and beckoned me. I thrive on them. I am indeed a bit of an intellectual wanderer, but I find doing the same thing again and again bores me. I wonder why people resist change and waste so much effort doing it when they can easily adapt—almost everything in today's world is idiot-proof and user-friendly!

I find it easier to go with the flow in most cases. From the bottom of my heart, I trust that all new and changing circumstances will end in amicable outcomes. Being an incurable optimist, I believe the universe will restore balance sooner rather than later.

This reminds me of the song 'Why Worry' by Dire Straits, which goes something like this:

> There should be laughter after pain
> There should be sunshine after rain
> These things have always been the same
> So why worry now?

Endnote

As you might have realised by now, I have been as candid about myself and my worldview as possible in this book. I may not have written about many things that truly worry me—my reckless past, my bleak future, and my ordinary present.

This is because I do not consider this book a reprieve, a game-changer, or a journal. It is simply a collection of random musings. I have consciously avoided airing my dirty linen in public because I choose to, and I have every right to do so.

Some of you might have enjoyed my choice of topics, my rendition, and my insights. Others may consider this book a waste of their time and money. Either way, I am certain you have discovered something in this book—however significant or minor its impact on your life. This book is sincere, not a revelation. Mind you, it takes courage to be honest about oneself, especially with strangers. I have lost much and have nothing more to lose.

I have tried to make the book fundamentally cheerful or 'amusingly morose'. When one is producing 50,000 words of content, one naturally becomes repetitive, contradictory, occasionally pedantic, and—at times—downright dull. My apologies.

I have made the language as simple and impactful as possible. I have used all my creative and imaginative abilities to make the book interesting, if not life-changing. It really does not matter to me whether your life changes after reading this book. What matters is whether you have become more curious about existential questions.

So, go ahead and script your itinerary for your journey of self-discovery. If, in that process, you recall or revisit something expressed in this book, or hark back to it and find yourself in agreement with it, I shall consider myself successful.

This is my debut, and for all I know, I may remain a one-book wonder and never write another. But trust me when I say this book has been a labour of love for me. I have never been happier than I am now.

People who know me may criticise me as a hypocrite when they read this book. That is anticipated. It only goes to show how misunderstood I am by those very people. Those who truly matter to me and genuinely know me will realise this book is the most important endeavour I have ever dared to undertake. They are happy for me and often tell me so. It is their kudos I seek, not everyone's.

At some point in the book, it is natural for you to assume I have been radical at times and very defensive at others. That is because that is how my mind functions—through highs and lows. I barely manage to remain sober and stable most of the time. Equanimity is a gift I am yet to receive. But in these magnificent highs and crippling lows are born the original ideas that make up this book.

Lastly, a big thank you! By reading this book, you have not saved me from another disappointment—you have made me happy. I wish you a joyful journey, too. If our paths ever cross, we will have something to talk about—your life and times.

Acknowledgements

I wish to thank my publisher, Hay House, for choosing to publish my book. Especially, Associate Editor Sonali Pawar for editing my book.

I wish to thank former colleague and friend Sumaa Tekur for handholding me and guiding me with the writing and publishing of this book.